COMPLETE ENGLISH

BOOK FOUR

COMPLETE ENGLISH

by

E. G. THORPE B.A.

Headmaster, The Margaret Wix Junior School
St. Albans

BOOK FOUR

Illustrated by

JOAN MILROY

HEINEMANN EDUCATIONAL BOOKS
LONDON

Heinemann Educational Books Ltd
LONDON EDINBURGH MELBOURNE AUCKLAND TORONTO
SINGAPORE HONG KONG KUALA LUMPUR
IBADAN NAIROBI JOHANNESBURG
LUSAKA NEW DELHI

ISBN 0 435 01888 4

First published 1962
Reprinted 1964, 1967, 1969, 1971, 1972, 1975

Published by Heinemann Educational Books Ltd,
48 *Charles Street, London, W1X* 8*AH*

This book has been printed in Great Britain by Brightype litho at Flarepath Printers Ltd, St. Albans, Herts.

Preface

This five-book English Course covers the following Junior School English: Comprehension, Language and Research (Spelling, Vocabulary, Dictionary work and Topics). It is intended for the consideration of teachers who believe that children come to school to work to the limit of their ability, that they should enjoy so doing through the provision of interesting work and that they should be encouraged to find out for themselves as far as possible by confident use of dictionary, atlas, reference books, etc.

Book IV is for 4th Year Junior quicker children and Lower Secondary forms. There are thirty exercises, each exercise being divided into three parts: Comprehension, Language and Find Out.

To allow facing-pages for the Comprehension passage and questions in the five-page exercises of Book IV, alternate exercises (the even-numbered ones) end with Comprehension, instead of beginning with it.

Comprehension has two sections: A (fairly easy) and B (more difficult). The aim has been to present interesting, well-written passages of prose and poetry from a wide variety of authors and to set questions which require thought on the pupil's part, many questions requiring deduction from facts stated in the passage. Where a simple Yes/No answer is required, children are asked to say how they know. Children should be asked to think of their own title for each extract.

Language arises as far as is reasonably possible from the Comprehension passage, each exercise having a main topic. The essential points of Grammar at this stage are covered, with constant revision throughout. Particular attention is given to common grammatical and spelling errors, to increased vocabulary and facility in the use of Language.

Find Out encourages children to use dictionary, atlas, reference books, etc., in finding out the meaning and use of words and phrases and in research on a topic suggested by the Comprehension passage. Extensions of questions found in the Language Section are included in this section, especially questions demanding research for which there would not be time in the Language lesson.

There are four sections: (i) The meaning and use of words. (ii) Colloquialisms, etc. (iii) Vocabulary research. (iv) Topic research, including history, geography, nature study, etc., in the belief that subjects should not be isolated.

Each exercise in Book IV ends with a list of books or poems recommended for further reading. It is felt that such lists are of special value at this stage.

The main topics dealt with in Parts II and III of each exercise are listed in summary form on the contents pages.

"Key to Complete English Book Four" is available, giving answers to the Comprehension and Language section, together with some additional notes.

Acknowledgments

Thanks are due to the following authors, or their representatives and publishers, for permission to quote copyright material:

Methuen & Co. Ltd. for *The Fight* from "The Wind in the Willows" by Kenneth Grahame.

George Allen & Unwin Ltd. and Messrs. Rand McNally for *A Long Voyage* from "The Kon-Tiki Expedition" by Thor Heyerdahl.

Laurence Pollinger Ltd. and the Estate of the late Mrs. Frieda Lawrence, for *The Injured Dog* from "Reflections on the Death of a Porcupine" by D. H. Lawrence, and *Poachers in Flight* from "The Poacher" by H. E. Bates.

Robert Hale Ltd. for *The Poachers* from "Chance Intruder" by E. G. Thorpe.

Clarendon Press for "London Snow" by Robert Bridges.

Cassell & Co. Ltd. for *A Peaceful Scene* from "King Solomon's Mines" by H. Rider Haggard.

Michael Joseph Ltd. for *Splash!* from "Jennie" by Paul Gallico.

Putnam & Co. Ltd. for "The Jervis Bay" by Michael Thwaites.

Oxford University Press for *An Unexpected Sight* from "Simon" by Rosemary Sutcliff; *Practice Makes Perfect* from "Sons of the Steppe" by Hans Baumann; *The Chase* from "The Eagle of the Ninth" by Rosemary Sutcliff, and "The Squirrel" by Ian Serraillier.

Hutchinson & Co. for *A Ruined City* from "Exploration Fawcett" by Lt.-Col. Fawcett.

Angus & Robertson Ltd. for *North of Kullaroo* from "Six and Silver" by Joan Phipson.

John Hunt: "The Ascent of Everest" based on the original despatches from Brigadier Sir John Hunt and other members of the Everest Expedition to *The Times*, and published by Hodder & Stoughton Ltd.

Collins for *Escaping* from "The Wooden Horse" by Eric Williams.

Mr. Siegfried Sassoon for "Morning Express".

Wells Gardner Darton & Co. Ltd. for *Chased by the Navy* from "Jim Davis" by John Masefield.

Hodder & Stoughton Ltd. and the Tweedsmuir Trustees for *Hunted by an Enemy* from "The Three Hostages" by John Buchan.

Contents

1 *The Fight*

What a squealing and a squeaking and a screeching filled the air!

Well might the terrified weasels dive under the tables and spring madly up at the windows! Well might the ferrets rush wildly for the fireplace and get hopelessly jammed in the chimney! Well might tables and chairs be upset, and glass and china be sent crashing on the floor, in the panic of that terrible moment when the four Heroes strode wrathfully into the room! The mighty Badger, his whiskers bristling, his great cudgel whistling through the air; Mole, black and grim, brandishing his stick and shouting his awful war-cry, "A Mole! A Mole!" Rat, desperate and determined, his belt bulging with weapons of every age and every variety; Toad, frenzied with excitement and injured pride, swollen to twice his ordinary size, leaping into the air and emitting Toad-whoops that chilled them to the marrow! "Toad he went a-pleasuring!" he yelled. "I'll pleasure 'em!" and he went straight for the Chief Weasel.

They were but four in all, but to the panic-stricken weasels the hall seemed full of monstrous animals, grey, black, brown, and yellow, whooping and flourishing enormous cudgels; and they broke and fled with squeals of terror and dismay, this way and that, through the windows, up the chimney, anywhere to get out of reach of those terrible sticks.

The affair was soon over. Up and down, the whole length of the hall, strode the four Friends, whacking with their sticks at every head that showed itself; and in five minutes the room was cleared. Through the broken windows the shrieks of terrified weasels escaping across the lawn were borne faintly to their ears; on the floor lay prostrate some dozen or so of the enemy, on whom the Mole was busily engaged in fitting handcuffs. The Badger, resting from his labours, leant on his stick and wiped his honest brow.

From *The Wind in the Willows* by Kenneth Grahame

Comprehension

A 1. How many animals strode into the room?
2. Who were they?
3. What was broken? Be careful or you will miss something.
4. Who tried to escape up the chimney?
5. Whom did Toad attack?
6. (a) Who yelled a battle-cry? (b) Why do you think he did this?
7. What was the chief weapon used?
8. How long did it take to defeat the enemy?
9. (a) Who made sure that some of the enemy did not escape? (b) How?
10. What is the meaning of: terrified, weasels, ferrets, mighty Badger, whooping, cudgel, whacking, handcuffs, brow?

Remember always: Use your dictionary.

B 1. (a) Why was there a squealing, squeaking and screeching?
(b) What is the difference between these noises?
2. Toad returned home to find weasels and ferrets living in his house, feasting and singing songs about him. How do we know that the songs annoyed him?
3. "The hall seemed full of monstrous animals, grey, black, brown, and yellow."
(a) What are "*monstrous* animals"? (b) Which animal fits each colour?
4. How could the hall seem "*full of* monstrous animals"?
5. Why do you think Toad attacked the *Chief* Weasel?
6. What tells us that the hall was a very large room?
7. (a) What does this mean: "The affair was soon over."?
(b) Why was it soon over?
8. What suggests that one animal was not tired at the end?
9. Put these phrases into your own words:
(i) frenzied with excitement (ii) lay prostrate (iii) resting from his labours.
10. What is the meaning of: hopelessly jammed, wrathfully, brandishing, flourishing, variety, emitting Toad-whoops, chilled to the marrow, went a-pleasuring, panic-stricken, busily engaged, his honest brow?

1 Language

1. What is an abbreviation?

   Remember: etc. (et cetera) means *and so on*: weasels, ferrets, stoats, etc.

2. PUNCTUATION What does *punctuation* mean? Why is it important?

   If you cannot answer the second question, try to give the meaning of this sentence:

   Is it time to go yet Uncle John asked

   Only punctuation will tell us WHO SPOKE:

   "Is it time to go yet, Uncle?" John asked.

   OR "Is it time to go yet?" Uncle John asked.

   Punctuation Marks ! ' " " — , . ( ) ?

   What do we call these eight punctuation marks? When is each one used?

   Two others which you will not often use are the colon (:) and the semi-colon (;).

   You will find the colon used often in these exercises, as a kind of *dash*.

   A semi-colon is a longer pause than a comma but it is a shorter pause than a full stop. Find examples in "The Fight".

   Remember:

   (1) Punctuation marks help to make the meaning clear.

   (2) Inverted commas showing that words have been copied from a book are called *Quotation marks:* "What a squealing and a squeaking and a screeching filled the air!"

   (3) Titles of books and poems, etc., have inverted commas: "The Wind in the Willows" by Kenneth Grahame; "The Squirrel" by Mary Howitt. Printers put titles in italics: *Oliver Twist* by Charles Dickens.

   Punctuate these sentences, remembering capital letters as well:

   (i) i enjoyed reading treasure island an adventure story by r l stevenson

   (ii) lie down the captain shouted cant you see its dangerous to stand up

   (iii) peter and joan thompson eleven years old and twins live in york road

3. The word Comprehension is the noun formed from the verb *to comprehend.*

   (i) What does the verb mean?

   (ii) What are the verbs formed from these nouns: terror, variety, pleasure?

4. Put into alphabetical order: enormous, awful, weasels, ferrets, stick, black, tables, cudgel, pride.

5. *Find the Stranger* squeal spring squeak screech

   Remember always: Say WHY one is a stranger.

6. Think of words which sound exactly the same but which are spelt differently:
   four (2), size, sent (2), aloud, alter, beach.
   Give the meaning of your words.
7. Put these words in order, beginning with the one which means "least afraid":
   (a) terror, fear, alarm, dismay.
   (b) frightened, terrified, alarmed, worried.
8. Put these words into interesting sentences of your own:
   terrified, terrible, various, variety.
9. "On the floor *lay* prostrate some dozen or so of the enemy. . . ."
   Do not confuse the two verbs "to lie down" and "to lay the table or eggs, etc.".
   Remember: (1) LIE means to tell a lie or to lie down NOW. Present tense.
   LAY means to put something down NOW. Present tense.
   I lie down when I am tired. I am going to lie down now.
   Lay down your arms and surrender!
   (2) I lie down now. I LAY down this morning (NOT now).
   LIE: Present tense. LAY: Past tense. *Note this carefully.*
   Write correctly:
   (i) (Lie, Lay) down and go to sleep.
   (ii) I was so tired, I (lay, lie) down and went to sleep.
   (iii) (Lie, Lay) the clean sheets carefully over there.
10. What are the opposites of pleasure, enormous, wrathfully, terrified, yelled?
11. Give words with the same meaning as terrified, panic, wrathfully, frenzied, sad.
12. *Spelling* (a) grassland: f. .ld (b) not an enemy: fr. . . . (c) good-looking: han. . . . . (d) dreadful: hor. . . . . (e) pause, waver: hes. . . . . (f) coal-mine: col. . . . . (g) very high hills: mou. . . . . . (h) ideas: tho. . . . . (i) describing words: adj. . . . . . . (j) He looks after sheep: she. . . . .
13. Think of ALL the meanings of these words, like LIE (to lie down; to tell a lie):
   well, might, tables, spring, jam, upset, glass, stick, cry, mole.
14. What do we mean by Parts of Speech?
   If you have forgotten, perhaps the two parts of speech in this list may remind you: speaking, inverted commas, nouns, capital letters, verbs, shout, work.
15. Use in five sentences: squealing squeaking screeching hopelessly jammed terrible moment.
   Remember always: Make your own sentences interesting.

Find Out

1. Find what these words mean, then use one from each group in sentences:
   emitting, omitting, permitting, transmitting   whistle, bristle, thistle
   wrath, wreath, wraith, wreck, wrench, wrestle, wretch, writhe
   squeal, squeak, squawk, squabble, scream, screech   pride, pried.

   Remember always: Many words have more than one meaning.
2. Find the meaning of: leapfrog, frogmarch, toady, toad-in-the-hole, badger someone, ferret out, caught like a rat in a trap, as grey as a badger, as blind as a mole, like a drowned rat, a badger-dog, Rats desert a sinking ship.
3. *Sounds* Make a list of animal and bird noises, like this: A snake hisses. A hurt dog yelps. A lonely dog howls.
4. *Six Wild Animals* Find out all you can about toads, rats, moles, badgers, weasels and ferrets. What are these: molehills, a mole's fortress, a set, ermine, dachshunds, tadpoles, "earth-pigs", Brock, nocturnal creatures?

   What is the connection between one of the six animals and the years 1348 and 1665?

Book List

The Wind in the Willows by Kenneth Grahame.
Toad of Toad Hall, a play by A. A. Milne.
Badger's Wood; Badger's Beech by Elleston Trevor.
The Observer's Book of Wild Animals of the British Isles by W. J. Stokoe.
The Observer's Book of Pond Life by John Clegg.
Wild Life Through the Year by Richard Morse.
Signposts to the Wild by E. D. Tinne.
Wild Animals in Britain by O. G. Pike.
The Wonderful Story of Living Things by Michael Gabb.

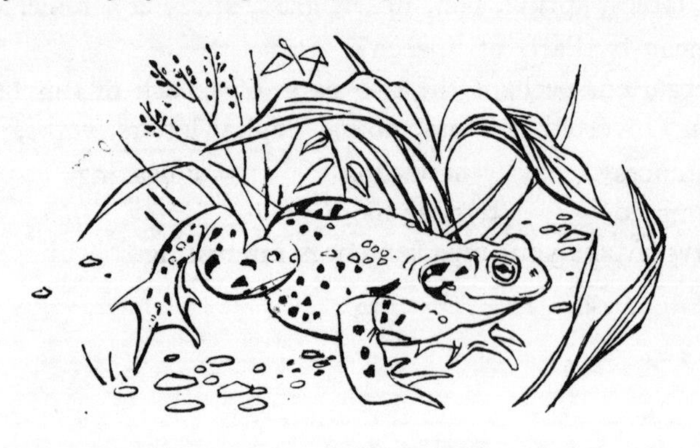

Comprehension comes at the end of this exercise.

2 Language

1. (a) Say what we call these punctuation marks and when we use them:
   ? ! . , ; : " " '

   (b) Punctuate, remembering capital letters as well:
   joris and i galloped on past looz tongres and dalhem suddenly joris shouted go on alone my horse can go no further

2. PARTS OF SPEECH

   All words can be put into groups according to their work: naming-words (nouns), doing-words or actions (verbs), describing-words (adjectives), etc.

   These groups are called Parts of Speech, eight in number:
   noun, pronoun, adjective, verb, adverb, preposition, conjunction, exclamation.

   When you learn a new word, always find out what part of speech it is, then see if there are any other parts of speech formed from that word, like this:

   (i) strength: noun (The *strength* of Samson).

   Other parts of speech: adjective: strong; adverb: strongly; verb: strengthen.

   (ii) please: verb (Dogs like *to please* their owners.)

   Other parts of speech: noun: pleasure; adjective: pleasant; adverb: pleasantly.

   Form other parts of speech from these words: sad, deepen, attractively, success.

3. (a) What is the difference between a cathedral, a church and a chapel?

   (b) What are these places or buildings: rookery, circus, laundry, orchard, gasometer or gas-holder, poultry farm, aquarium, orphanage, cemetery, barracks?

4. ". . who *brought* good news from Ghent."

   Do not confuse the two verbs *brought* and *bought*.

   *Remember: br*ought goes with *br*ing, *b*ought goes with *b*uy.

   Write these sentences correctly:

   (i) He went to the book-shop and (bought, brought) "Treasure Island".

   (ii) Mother (bought, brought) my supper up to my bedroom.

5. " '*Neath* our feet . . . . his head '*twixt* my knees on the ground"

   (a) What do the two abbreviations mean?
   What does the apostrophe show?

   (b) What do these abbreviations mean: o'clock, o'er, she'll, can't, it's?

6. (a) Which words in the Comprehension poem rhyme with three, through, chaff and Ghent?

   (b) Which of these words rhymes with GRIEF: great, greet, leaf, believe?

7. Put into alphabetical order: stirrup, gallop, three, wall, watch, sprang, was.

8. Think of words which sound exactly the same but which are spelt differently: night, past, sun, wine, due, berry, board, bolder.

   Give the meaning of your words.

9. *Find the Stranger* sprang galloped sank laughed ran

10. Give the opposite of shut, sank, broad, laugh, beneath, remember, praise, push.

11. *Horses* What do we call these: a male horse, a female horse, a very young (baby) horse, a young male and a young female horse, their home and a man who rides racehorses?

12. *Spelling* (a) a bird: pig... (b) a pain in the head: hea..... (c) not quietly: noi.... (d) very clever: ski.... (e) at once: im......... (f) out of breath: bre....... (g) vanish: dis...... (h) horrible: gha.... (i) the start: beg...... (j) not the same: dif......

13. Write down the title of a book which you have read, the author's name and a sentence about the story.

14. Use in sentences: bolt (i. a noun; ii. two different verbs); till (i. a noun; ii. a verb).

15. What is Direct Speech? Write down an example.

16. Use in five sentences: midnight a pitiless laugh good news we galloped all I remember.

Find Out

1. Find what these words mean, then use one from each group in sentences:
   sprang, sprain, sprawl, spray, spread, sprout, spruce, sprung, spring
   gallop, gallon, galley, galleon, gallery, gallant, gallows
   watch, witch, which, watchful, wasteful
   through, threw, throughout, threw out.

2. Find the meaning of: a horse's walk, trot, canter, gallop; three figures, the three R's, threescore years and ten; Two's company, three's a crowd; play at sight, know someone by sight, lose sight of something, on sight; out of sight, out of mind; sight-seeing, sightless.

3. *Movement* Make a list of verbs of movement and suitable "doers" of the action, like this: A horse gallops. A baby crawls. A fox prowls.

4. *Famous Rides* Find out the title of the Comprehension poem. It begins: "How They Brought the Good News . . ."

Find out about famous rides (fact and fiction), like Dick Turpin's Ride to York; the Charge of the Light Brigade; the Rides of Paul Revere, Mazeppa, John Gilpin, Tschiffely, etc.

What have these to do with famous rides: Mancha and Gato, Black Bess, Edmonton, Cossacks, minutemen, Crimea, the highwayman Nevinson, cannons?

List of Poems

How They Brought the Good News from Ghent to Aix by Robert Browning.
The Charge of the Light Brigade by Tennyson.
John Gilpin by William Cowper.
Paul Revere's Ride by H. W. Longfellow.
Mazeppa by Byron.
The Highwayman; The Ballad of Dick Turpin by Alfred Noyes.
Windy Nights by Robert Louis Stevenson.
The Knight's Leap by Charles Kingsley.
The Smuggler's Leap by R. H. Barham.
The Cavalier's Escape by G. W. Thornbury.

2 *Three Horsemen*

I sprang to the stirrup, and Joris, and he;
I galloped, Dirck galloped, we galloped all three;
"Good speed!" cried the watch, as the gate-bolts undrew;
"Speed!" echoed the wall to us galloping through;
Behind shut the postern, the lights sank to rest,
And into the midnight we galloped abreast.

. . . .

So we were left galloping, Joris and I,
Past Looz and past Tongres, no cloud in the sky;
The broad sun above laughed a pitiless laugh,
'Neath our feet broke the brittle bright stubble like chaff;
Till over by Dalhem a dome-spire sprang white,
And "Gallop," gasped Joris, "for Aix is in sight!"

. . . .

And all I remember is, friends flocking round
As I sat with his head 'twixt my knees on the ground,
And no voice but was praising this Roland of mine,
As I poured down his throat our last measure of wine,
Which (the burgesses voted by common consent)
Was no more than his due who brought good news from Ghent.

These are the first, seventh and tenth (the last) verses of a poem by Robert Browning.

Comprehension

A

1. How many men are there?
2. How are they travelling?
3. What are their names, if given?
4. Who bade them farewell?
5. How did they gallop at first: one behind the other, one a long way ahead of the others, level with one another, one a long way behind?
6. What time did they set out?
7. What was the weather like at Looz and Tongres: sunny, cloudy, stormy, wet?
8. Read the poem aloud. Can you hear a special rhythm? What does it suggest?
9. What happened to the last drink of wine?
10. What is the meaning of: stirrup, gate-bolts, echoed, the lights sank to rest, pitiless, brittle, stubble, chaff, gasped, flocking round, praising?

B

1. (a) To which city did the men wish to ride? (b) From which city?
2. Who reached the end of the journey? Write *man* or *horse* after their names.
3. (a) Why did they go? (b) What do you think the "good news" was?
4. How can you tell that this did not happen in our country?
5. How can you tell that this happened long ago?
6. What does this line reveal:
   "So we were left galloping, Joris and I"?
7. Describe this scene:
   "I sat with his head 'twixt my knees on the ground"
8. (a) Where do you think the person "I" lived? (b) Why do you think so?
9. Why did everyone praise Roland?
10. What is the meaning of: sprang to the stirrup, the watch, postern, a pitiless laugh, a dome-spire sprang white, the burgesses (citizens) voted by common consent, no more than his due, "Good speed!"?

3

Accused of Theft

The offence had been committed within the district, and indeed in the immediate neighbourhood, of a very notorious metropolitan police officer. The crowd had only the satisfaction of accompanying Oliver through two or three streets, and down a place called Mutton-hill, when he was led beneath a low archway, and up a dirty court, into this dispensary of summary justice, by the back way. It was a small paved yard into which they turned; and here they encountered a stout man with a bunch of whiskers on his face and a bunch of keys in his hand.

"What's the matter now?" said the man carelessly.

"A young fogle-hunter," replied the man who had Oliver in charge.

"Are you the party that's been robbed, sir?" inquired the man with the keys.

"Yes, I am," replied the old gentleman; "but I am not sure that this boy actually took the handkerchief. I—I would rather not press the case."

"Must go before the magistrate now, sir," replied the man. "His worship will be disengaged in half a minute. Now, young gallows."

This was an invitation for Oliver to enter through a door which he unlocked as he spoke, and which led into a stone cell. Here he was searched, and nothing being found upon him, locked up.

From *Oliver Twist* by Charles Dickens

Comprehension

A 1. Who went with Oliver and the man who was taking him to the police court?

2. Was Oliver taken in by the front, side or back door?
3. Where did they meet the man with the keys?
4. Describe that man.
5. Complete this: The man with the keys was (annoyed, angry, pleasant, unconcerned).
6. What question did this man ask?
7. What answer was given?
8. Why was an old gentleman there?
9. What happened to Oliver after the man with the keys had unlocked a door?
10. What is the meaning of: neighbourhood, neighbour, crowd, archway, paved, whiskers, a bunch of keys, had . . . in charge, actually?

B 1. Why did the old gentleman *stammer* "I—I would . . ."?

2. What is the district of a police officer?
3. (a) Why do you think a crowd went with Oliver?
   (b) Explain: ". . . had only the satisfaction of accompanying Oliver."
4. Give in your own words the route taken.
5. (a) Who would the man with the keys be? (b) What is a magistrate?
6. Why should Oliver be called "young gallows"?
7. (a) What was Oliver invited to do? (b) Was it really an invitation?
   (c) What would YOU call it?
8. What does the adjective *notorious* tell us about the police officer?
9. Use your dictionary to try to explain this difficult word: metropolitan; and this difficult phrase: dispensary of summary justice.
10. What is the meaning of: offence, committed, immediate neighbourhood, encountered, fogle-hunter, Are you the party . . .? I would rather not press the case, will be disengaged?

3 *Language*

1. What are the eight Parts of Speech?
   Form verbs from these nouns: fright, depth, resolution, thought.
2. DIRECT SPEECH "What's the matter now?" said the man carelessly.
   The actual words spoken, written down inside inverted commas: Direct Speech.
   Remember: (1) Full stops, commas, question and exclamation marks go inside the closing inverted commas:
   "I would like to help you," he said. "May I try?"
   (2) Always close the inverted commas when one person stops speaking; always open new ones *on the next line* when someone else starts to speak:
   "May I go fishing with you?" asked the boy.
   "I'm sorry I can't take you today," replied his father.

   INDIRECT SPEECH The man asked carelessly what was the matter.
   The actual words spoken are not given so there are no inverted commas.
   Remember: Do not use apostrophe-abbreviations in Indirect Speech:
   The climbers couldn't reach the summit of the mountain. WRONG
   The climbers could not reach the summit of the mountain. RIGHT

   (a) Change to Indirect Speech:
   (i) "This is the way," I said to my friends.
   (ii) "I'm afraid I'm lost," said the stranger.
   (b) Change to Direct Speech:
   (iii) The park-keeper told the children that the swing was not safe.
   (iv) The small boy asked his mother to tell him a story.
   (c) Why is Indirect Speech also called Reported Speech?
3. *Find the Stranger* policeman architect library plumber doctor
4. Think of words which sound exactly the same but which are spelt differently: been, place, led, court, keys, boy, border, bough, break, bridle.
   Give the meaning of your words.
5. Put into alphabetical order: offence, commit, district, crowd, way, court, satisfaction, handkerchief, chief, cell.
6. *Spelling* (a) Past tense of *fight*: f..... (b) not brave: cow..... (c) brave: cou....... (d) a shortened word: abb......... (e) above your head: c...... (f) happened: occ..... (g) in arms and legs: mus.... (h) words

ending in the same sound: r..mes (i) not innocent: g..... (j) a shout: exc........

7. Use in sentences: down (noun) low (verb) yard (two nouns)
8. What are ALL the meanings of left, rose, pine, brood, ground, stamp, foot, bound?
9. Make the second pair agree in the same way that the first pair agree.
   Here is an example: wood, forest : hill, MOUNTAIN; because a forest is a large wood, a large hill is a *mountain*.

house, people	:	rookery, ——
mutton, sheep	:	——, calf
bunch, keys	:	bouquet, ——
gentleman, lady	:	——, duchess
chimney, chimneys	:	piano, ——
tiny, enormous	:	attack, ——
possible, impossible	:	legal, ——
in, out	:	interior, ——
come, came	:	shake, ——
spring, summer	:	——, winter

10. What is the plural of: yard, policeman, police station, archway, arch, party, boy, handkerchief, minute, gentleman?
11. What is the difference in meaning between: to commit a crime, to commit to prison; to be in charge, to have in charge, to charge (2)?
12. Write this correctly:
    oliver twist was accused of stealing an old gentlemans handkerchief you may wonder why anyone should want to steal a handkerchief it was because they were valuable in those days we can read all about it in oliver twist by charles dickens
13. Use these two joining-words in one sentence: but, because.
14. What is a noun? What are Common and Proper nouns?
    Make two lists (i) Common (ii) Proper nouns, found in this sentence:
    In the book "Oliver Twist" by Charles Dickens, we read about a gang of thieves and robbers in London many years ago.
15. Use in five sentences: beneath a low archway a bunch of keys an invitation a stone cell neighbourhood.

Find Out

1. Find what these words mean, then use one from each group in sentences:
   very, verify, vertical, horizontal — commit, permit, admit, submit
   notorious, famous, eminent, popular — streets, straits, straight
   offence, defence — arch, larch, march, March, parched, starch
   minute (noun), minute (adjective).
2. Find the meaning of: down at heel, down in the mouth, down on one's luck, down and out, Down Under, down on someone, go down, ups and downs, downcast, the down line and platform, downfall, downhill, downpour, downstairs; keyboard, key-note, key-cold, key-ring, keystone, keyed-up.
3. *Speaking* Make a list of verbs of speaking and describe each one, like this: stammer: to falter or stutter; mumble: to speak indistinctly.
4. *Police* Find out all you can about the history of the Police, crime and punishment. Who or what were these: the Watch, Bow Street Runners, whipping-posts, stocks, pillories, ducking-stools, curfew, manor courts, sheriffs, ordeal by fire, gibbets, prison-hulks, "bobbies" and "Peelers"?

Book List

Oliver Twist; Great Expectations; David Copperfield by Charles Dickens.
Emil and the Detectives by Erich Kastner.
A Hundred Million Francs by Paul Berna.
The Police and Crime Detection Today by Reginald Morrish.
The Arm of the Law by G. A. Campbell.
The Policeman by Nicholas Bebbington.
The True Book about Scotland Yard by Leonard Gribble.
Serving One Another by W. J. Weston.
The Policeman by Vera Southgate and J. Havenhand.
Law and Order by John Dumpleton.

Comprehension comes at the end of this exercise.

4 *Language*

1. Change to Direct Speech:
   I asked Teka to translate my speech into the Polynesian language.
2. Change into Indirect Speech:
   "I've been to many other islands in the Pacific Ocean," I said to the native chief.
3. NOUNS What is a noun? What are Common and Proper nouns?
   How can we recognise a Proper noun?
   Find five different Proper nouns in the Comprehension passage, "A Long Voyage", then find the same number of Common nouns.
   What are the nouns formed from these words, like *bravery* from the adjective brave : educated, intelligent, mysterious, distant, descended, believe, repeated, excited, disappeared, speak?
   Remember: (1) If you are not sure whether a word is a noun or not, put THE in front of it and if it is a Common noun it will make sense, like this:
   fog, foggy : The fog (makes sense: NOUN)
   The foggy (not finished, nonsense: not a noun)
   (2) While it is easy to recognise pen, ink, man, dog, wood, etc. as nouns, you may have trouble in recognising these words as nouns:
   poverty, satisfaction, courage, friendship, happiness, etc.
   These are not the names of real objects which can be seen or touched but they are still nouns because they are naming-words: the names of qualities or feelings: the poverty of the people, the satisfaction which I felt, the courage, etc. Such nouns are called ABSTRACT nouns.
   Write down six more abstract nouns.
4. *Find the Stranger* Pacific Atlantic Irish Sea Ireland Red Sea
5. Put into alphabetical order: wait, brown, speak, them, brought, believe, assembly, their, been, chief, before, bought.
6. *bring* and *fetch:* bring something: come with it
   fetch something: go for it
   Say what is the difference in meaning between these two statements:

(i) I will bring the children home at eight o'clock.
(ii) I will fetch the children home at eight o'clock.
Use *bring* and *fetch* in two sentences.

7. Use these words in sentences: whose, who's.
8. Give the opposite of: high, first, forefathers, no one, distant, descended (a mountain), believe, visible, probable, coloured.
9. "It was an *uneducated* . . . gathering . . ."
The prefix *un* at the front of *educated* gives us the opposite of that word.
Put prefixes at the front of these words to make opposites:
happy, satisfied, possible, visible, sense, legal, regular, safe, arrange, probable, direct, willing.
10. Give words which mean the same as these: sprang, intelligent, a gathering of people, mysterious, distant, mighty, a number of, disappeared, constantly, repeated.
11. Write this correctly:
the first chief whose name was kon-tiki brought a group of his people out of peru in south america to the south sea islands in the pacific ocean where they settled down whos going to tell us about their exciting voyage i said
12. *Spelling* (a) a low muttering: m.r..r (b) our next door n....bours (c) screaming: shr...... (d) marvellous: won...... (e) joy: ple..... (f) blowing shrilly: w..st.... (g) moving like a thief: ste.....ly (h) on the roads: traf... (i) go with someone: acc...... (j) on time: pun.....
13. Put in the missing words:

Present tense	*Simple Past tense*	*Past tense with "have", etc.*
I hear	I heard	I have heard
——	——	He had brought
——	He sprang	——
John swims	——	——
Susan writes	——	——

14. Use in sentences: *light*: (i) as a verb, (ii) as a noun, (iii) and (iv) as two different adjectives.
15. What is an adjective? Write a sentence containing three (underlined).
16. Use in five sentences: a mysterious country fire and flame a number of sprang forward embarrassed.

Find Out

1. Find what these words mean, then use one from each group in sentences:
   quiet, quite, requite, require, acquire, acquit   arms, armour, alms
   farther, father, further   weather, whether   mysterious, mischievous
   beach, beech, beaker, breakers, beacon   assemble, reassemble, resemble.
2. Find the meaning of: all at sea, find one's sea-legs, follow the sea for a living, a sea-calf, sea-canary, sea-dog, sea-fox, sea-elephant, sea-cow, sea-horse, sea-lion, sea-rat, sea-wolf; someone's life hangs by a thread, lose or pick up the thread of an argument, thread a needle, thread one's way, threadbare.
3. *Parts of Speech* Choose ten words from "A Long Voyage" and form other parts of speech from them, like this: fire (noun): fiery (adjective); fierily (adverb); to fire (verb).
4. *The South Sea Islands* Find Peru in South America in your atlas and on the globe, then the South Sea Islands in the Pacific Ocean. See how many different routes you can find for sea-cruises from one to the other, noting any islands or countries where the ship might call.

   Where in your atlas or on the globe can you find these names and what are they: Solomon, Gilbert, Caroline, Mariana, Cook, Marshall?

Book List

The Kon-Tiki Expedition by Thor Heyerdahl.
The Boy Who Was Afraid, Lost Lagoon by Armstrong Sperry.
The Raft by Kurt Schmeltzer.
Son of Columbus; The Barque of the Brothers by Hans Baumann.
The Early Explorers by Isabel Barclay.
They Put Out to Sea by Roger Duvoisin.
A Book of Discovery by M. B. Synge.
Exploring the Pacific by L. F. Hobley.
True Adventures Great Explorers Told Me by Betty Ross.
Six Great Explorers by David Divine.
Inoke Sails the South Seas by Ronald Rose.

4 *A Long Voyage*

Then Tupuhoe asked me to say a few words to the people as to why we had come across the sea on a *pae-pae*; they had all been counting on this. I was to speak in French, and Teka would translate bit by bit.

It was an uneducated, but highly intelligent gathering of brown people that stood waiting for me to speak. I told them that I had been among their kinsmen out here in the South Sea islands before, and that I had heard of their first chief, Tiki, who had brought their forefathers out to the islands from a mysterious country whose whereabouts no one knew any longer. But in a distant land called Peru, I said, a mighty chief had once ruled whose name was Tiki. The people called him Kon-Tiki, or Sun-Tiki, because he said he was descended from the Sun. Tiki and a number of followers had at last disappeared from their country on big *pae-paes*; therefore we six thought that he was the same Tiki who had come to those islands. As nobody would believe that a *pae-pae* could make the voyage across the sea, we ourselves had set out from Peru on a *pae-pae*, and here we were, so it could be done.

When the little speech was translated by Teka, Tupuhoe was all fire and flame, and sprang forward in front of the assembly in a kind of ecstasy. He rumbled away in Polynesian, flung out his arms, pointed to heaven and us, and in his flood of speech constantly repeated the word Tiki. He talked so fast that it was impossible to follow the thread of what he said, but the whole assembly swallowed every word and was visibly excited. Teka, on the contrary, looked quite embarrassed when he had to translate.

From *The Kon-Tiki Expedition* by Thor Heyerdahl

a *pae-pae*: a raft.

Comprehension

A 1. What did the natives wish to know?
2. What were the names of two of the natives there?
3. In which language was the story of the voyage told by one of the sailors?
4. What was the name of the first chief of the natives?
5. What is the name of the first land where Tiki was a great ruler?
6. How many people believed that Tiki had come from that distant country?
7. What was another name for Kon-Tiki and why was he given it?
8. (a) Who became very excited? (b) Why do you think he did this?
9. Where was this meeting: in Peru, on a South Sea island, in France, on a raft?
10. What is the meaning of: gathering, chief, islands, mysterious, mighty, whereabouts, disappeared, distant, ruled, followers, voyage, speech, French?

B 1. (a) What would nobody believe? (b) Can you think why?
2. (a) Why had six men made a long voyage? (b) How had they travelled?
3. Why do you think they called their voyage *The Kon-Tiki Expedition*?
4. Why must Teka have been very clever?
5. Why do you think the raft had such a strange name: a pae-pae?
6. (a) Who looked confused and uncomfortable? (b) Can you think why he did?
7. Why do you think Tiki and many followers had left Peru?
8. Make a list of all the speakers in the correct order.
9. Explain this: "an uneducated, but highly intelligent gathering".
10. What is the meaning of: been counting on this, kinsmen, forefathers, descended from the Sun, all fire and flame, rumbled away in Polynesian, flood of speech, impossible to follow the thread, swallowed every word, visibly excited, constantly repeated, translate, assembly, ecstasy, on the contrary?

5 *The Injured Dog*

I went out. And in the full blaze of sunlight in the field, stood two dogs, a black-and-white, and a big, bushy, rather handsome sandy-red dog, of the collie type. And sure enough this latter did look queer and a bit horrifying, his whole muzzle set round with white spines, like some ghastly growth; like an unnatural beard.

The black-and-white dog made off as I went through the fence. But the red dog whimpered and hesitated, and moved on hot bricks. He was fat and in good condition. I thought he might belong to some shepherds herding sheep in the forest ranges, among the mountains.

He waited while I went up to him, wagging his tail and whimpering, and ducking his head, and dancing. He daren't rub his nose with his paws any more; it hurt too much. I patted his head and looked at his nose, and he whimpered loudly.

He must have had thirty quills, or more, sticking out of his nose, all the way round: the white, ugly ends of the quills protruding an inch, sometimes more, sometimes less, from his already swollen, blood-puffed muzzle.

From *Reflections on the Death of a Porcupine* by D. H. Lawrence

Comprehension

A 1. Which dog looked very strange?
2. Which dog ran away?
3. What were the white spines?
4. What were the "hot bricks"?
5. Give an adjective to describe the weather.
6. Why did the dog not rub its nose?
7. What was the dog's "blood-puffed muzzle"?
8. (a) Who were the probable owners of the dog? (b) Where were they?
9. Which English wild animal is like the one which had hurt the dog?
10. What is the meaning of: handsome, queer, beard, whimpered, hesitated, shepherd, ghastly?

B 1. Where was the writer just before the extract begins?
2. (a) When did the unharmed dog run away? (b) Why do you think he ran away?
3. Why did the sandy-red dog look peculiar?
4. Which of these adjectives describe it: plump, thin, well-fed, undernourished, happy, worried?
5. What do you think the sandy-red dog had been doing?
6. What is this type of dog used for? There is a clue in the extract.
7. Why were the quill-ends white?
8. (a) What time of day do you think it is in this extract? (b) Why do you think so?
9. Which adjective describes the person: lazy, callous, sympathetic, handsome?
10. Explain: in the full blaze of sunlight, a bit horrifying, like some ghastly growth, like an unnatural beard, in good condition, forest ranges, ducking his head and dancing; protruding an inch, sometimes more, sometimes less; reflections on the death of a porcupine.

5 *Language*

1. Form nouns from (i) these adjectives: sad, ugly, horrible, painful, excited (ii) these verbs: grow, marry, serve, prosper, pursue.

2. ADJECTIVES What is an adjective?
Find six in the extract "The Injured Dog".

Remember: Adjectives DESCRIBE. Always try to think of interesting, descriptive adjectives for your Creative Writing.
Do not write "a nice red dog" when you can easily think of "a handsome, sandy-red dog".

(a) Here are some descriptive adjectives with poor or weak ones in brackets: terror-stricken, terrified or panic-stricken (afraid); agile, swift or nimble (quick); amusing, humorous (funny); amazed, astounded, bewildered, thunderstruck, baffled, mystified (puzzled); ancient (very old); enraged, irate, infuriated (angry); boisterous, thundering (noisy); cloudy, gloomy, dismal (dull); brilliant, dazzling, glittering, radiant, sparkling, twinkling (bright); huge, enormous, gigantic, colossal (very big); frosty, icy (cold); fierce, ferocious, vicious (nasty).

(b) Think of better adjectives instead of these:
nice-smelling, nice-tasting, nice-looking, nice-sounding, a *nice* walk, a *nice* cottage, a *nice* person, a *nice* story, a *nice* day.

(c) Use these adjectives in sentences:
reckless, fearless, disastrous, relentless, raucous.

3. *Find the Stranger* wagging whimpering ducking dancing

4. Find three different meanings of *muzzle*, then use one in a sentence.

5. Think of words which sound exactly the same but which are spelt differently: whole, wholly, some, to, paws, ceiling, seller, cereal, choir, course.
Give the meaning of your words.

6. *Spelling* (a) A horse running fast: gal...... (b) opposite of weeping: la...... (c) deserving pity: pit.... (d) and (e) the nouns from *long* and *broad* (f) many kinds: var.... (g) dreadful: ter..... (h) very frightened: ter...... (i) in despair: des...... (j) recall to mind: rem.....

7. Put into alphabetical order: any, as, and, ass, at, a, ash, all, an, among.

8. What are the father, mother and young ones of these families: foxes, fowls, ducks, tigers, lions, geese, cats?

9. Change to Direct Speech:
   (i) I asked the dog what was the matter with it.
   (ii) The shepherds told me that they had lost a collie and asked if I had seen one.
   (iii) The angry farmer ordered the trespassers to leave his land at once.

10. Give the plural of: field, I, collie, sheep, winch, chimney, thief.

11. Put in the missing words:
   (a) I saw a black-and-white dog —— ran away when I whistled.
   (b) I saw an old shepherd —— was looking for a lost ewe.
   (c) I looked everywhere for the lost dog —— could not find it.
   (d) I hurried to school —— I knew I was late.

12. Make the second pair agree in the same way that the first pair agree:

spider, fly	:	cat, ——
black, white	:	quick, ——
leg, foot	:	——, hand
Monday, Tuesday	:	January, ——
sheep, flock	:	cows, ——
man, woman	:	prince, ——
garden, fence	:	picture, ——
London, England	:	Dublin, ——

13. What do these words mean: single, double, treble?

14. What are verbs? Write a sentence and underline the verb in it.

15. Use in five sentences: whimpered loudly in the forest blaze hesitated reflections.

Find Out

1. Find what these words mean, then use one from each group in sentences:
   blaze, ablaze, blazer, blade, blare, blame collie, collier, colliery, college through, thorough, though, thought latter, later protrude, intrude loudly, lounge, lounger, lunge, plunge ghastly, ghostly, aghast.

2. Find the meaning of: to dog someone's footsteps, a dog in the manger, a dog's life, dog-tired, raining cats and dogs, the under-dog, top-dog, a hang-dog look, dog-fox, the Dog Star, the dog-watch, dog-roses, Every dog has his day. Give a dog a bad name and hang him. Let sleeping dogs lie.

3. *Unusual Colours* Make a list of unusual colours, then use each one in a sentence, like this: The soldiers were wearing *khaki* uniform.
4. *Dogs* (i) Make a list of different breeds and say what special use any of them have, like collies (sheep-dogs).
   (ii) Find out about famous dogs. Why are these dogs famous: Gelert, Rin-Tin-Tin (the original or first one died in 1932), Lassie, Barry the St. Bernard?
   What have these to do with dogs: "hare", Old English, Sheepdog Trials, Llewellyn, fox-hunting, Beddgelert, avalanches, husky, John Bull, escaped convicts, blind people?

Book List

Taff the Sheepdog; Son of Taff; Joker the Foxhound by Judith M. Berrisford.
Toyon, a Dog of the North by Nicholas Kalashnikoff.
The Hundred and One Dalmatians by Dodie Smith.
Kelpie, a Scottish Sheepdog by Cecilia Knowles.
Bellman the Beagle by K. F. Barker.
The Secret Dog by D. P. Thompson.
A Boy and Five Huskies by René Guillot.
City Dog by Gerald Raftery.
Dogs as Pets for Boys and Girls by C. E. G. Hope.
The Observer's Book of Dogs by C. B. Hubbard.
Dogs, Dogs, Dogs edited by Phyllis R. Fenner.
Working Dogs by Carol Odell.
Greatheart by Joseph E. Chipperfield.

Comprehension comes at the end of this exercise.

6 *Language*

1. Think of suitable adjectives to describe an ache, a wood, a warren, branches, rain.
2. VERBS What is a verb? Give an example, putting it in a sentence.

   Although most verbs tell us about actions, some do not: seem, become, feel, be (am, is, was, were, etc.):

   I am hungry. Charles became king. Jill felt ill. He seems better now.

   Verbs have *tenses* to tell us WHEN the action took place:

   Present tense I sing I am singing He runs She blushes It flies

   Past tense I sang I was singing I have sung I had sung He has sung

   Future tense I shall sing I shall be singing You will sing

   (1) Say which tense each verb is in: they were arguing, he is noisy, we shall come early, she has gone, he watches, it cries, I blew, you wrote.

   (2) *Present tense* Give the correct ending of each verb in brackets: she (run), he (watch), it (dry), I am (run), they are (come), we are (go), pigeons are (race), thieves are (rob), I am (taste), you are (sing), you are (singe).
3. *Find the Stranger* rustling slippery patter squeak yell
4. Think of words which sound exactly the same but which are spelt differently: wood, hear, rain, stare, see, passed, died, heard, caught, creak.

   Give the meaning of your words.
5. "*Kee--per!*" This is an exclamation or interjection. Remember that exclamation marks always go inside the inverted commas:

   He yelled "Kee--per!" at the top of his voice. NOT "Kee--per"!

   Complete these exclamations:

   "Look out yelled the fireman. "Stop shouted the policeman.
6. What are the masculine and feminine of the following: rabbits, cattle, deer, royalty (i. adults ii. children), pigs, grandparents, people?
7. Think of words which have the same meaning as noise, ache, tiny, stopped, close to, to close, yell, lovely, lively, gay.
8. Write correctly:

   (i) my name is dick turpin said the highwayman oh said the stranger is that supposed to frighten me to death

   (ii) go away shouted the shepherd angrily cant you see youre scaring the sheep

9. What is the difference between a hutch, burrow, rabbit-hole and warren?
10. What nouns are formed from turned, hear, run, passed, lose, touched, appear?
11. Change to Indirect Speech:
    (i) "Why did you let the gamekeeper catch us?" Ginger asked Peter angrily.
    (ii) "It was so dark that I didn't see him coming," replied Peter.
12. Put into alphabetical order: cat, cart, cab, catch, castle, cabbage, cattle.
13. *Spelling* (a) full of hope: hop.... (b) and (c) two shrill noises: scr...... and scr....... (d) without pity: pit..... (e) find the size: mea.... (f) brave men: her... (g) brave women: her..... (h) a nose-cloth: hand........ (i) taking care: car.... (j) a designer of buildings: arc......
14. Use in sentences: *sound* (i) as a noun (ii) as a verb (iii) as an adjective.
15. Make the second pair agree in the same way that the first pair agree:

thief, policeman	:	poacher, ——
appear, disappear	:	satisfied, ——
inside, outside	:	interior, ——
rabbits, warren	:	squirrels, ——
mouse, squeaks	:	elephant, ——
cattle, beef	:	sheep, ——
train, platform	:	ship, ——
go down, descend	:	climb, ——

16. Use in five sentences: slippery the patter of rain disappeared "Kee--per!" up in the branches.

Find Out

1. Find what these words mean, then use one from each group in sentences:
   treetops, top trees, in threes again, a gain, against along, a long way
   slippery, slipper, slipping, slipshod, slapping, slopping, sloping, sloop
   patter, pattern, patron, spatter, scatter, splatter close to, to close, a close.
2. Find the meaning of: with all one's heart, at heart, heart in mouth, heart-broken, know by heart, a change of heart, speak from the heart, heart of gold, a heavy heart, lose heart, set one's heart on it, sick at heart, with sinking heart, heart of stone, sweetheart, hearts of oak, the heart of the matter.
3. *Looking* Make a list of verbs of looking and describe each one, like this: stare: to look hard or fixedly at; glower: to look angrily at.

4. *Nocturnal Creatures* Find out about creatures which come out at night: bats, otters, foxes, badgers, owls, hedgehogs, etc.

What are these and with which creature are they connected: echo-location, pipistrelle, Tawny, Short-eared, holts, sets, earths, hovers, vixens, quadrupeds, M.F.H., the Shires, the Quorn, "bats' radar"?

Book List

The Boy's Country Book, edited by John Moore.
Getting to Know British Wild Animals by David Stephen.
The Children's Nature Book (Odhams).
The Young Field Naturalist's Guide by Maxwell Knight.
Animals of Britain by Edward Osmond.
Tracks, Trails and Signs by F. J. S. Speakman.
Wild Animals of the British Isles by Maurice Burton.
The Observer's Book of Birds by S. Vere Benson.
The Running Foxes by Joyce Stranger.
The Countryside by J. C. Gagg.

6 *The Poachers*

He turned his head at a sound in the wood, a rustling, a movement, grass slippery underfoot, a bird, a wood-pigeon, a twig blown off a tree, a rabbit . . . what? What was it?

He listened and listened, breathless, in one vast ache to hear. Again. And again. Like the patter of rain blown out of treetops. He stared and stared. What was it? The wood was full of tiny sounds: he could not run to Ginger at the squeak of a mouse or thump of a rabbit. Had it stopped? Ears, listen! Hear something! Stare, eyes, stare! See something; anything!

The man passed so close to him on the other side of the tree that if he had leaned out he could have touched him. At the sight of him Peter's heart froze into a tiny screwed-up ball and died. He could do nothing but stare at the man's back as he disappeared along the edge of the wood, heading towards the warren: a keeper with a gun under his arm, headed towards the gang and all Peter could do was stare after him.

Why hadn't he heard him? Which way had he come? That noise in the wood . . . there it was again! A twig snapping. Someone else. Another. He had been caught out. Listening to one, deaf to another. Quick, quick!

He cupped his hands to his mouth and yelled "Kee-per!" at the top of his voice and almost as he did so a gun went off in the direction of the warren and he heard a rush of shot up in the branches like rain, then Ginger yelling and the sound in the wood: someone running full-pelt towards him.

From *Chance Intruder* by E. G. Thorpe

keeper: an abbreviation of gamekeeper.

Comprehension

A 1. What was the name of the person who heard a noise?
2. What was damp, making walking difficult?
3. (a) Was it raining? (b) How do you know?
4. Who was the man and what was he carrying?
5. Where was the gun which was fired?
6. What snapped somewhere in the wood?
7. (a) Did Peter try to touch the man as he walked past? (b) How do you know?
8. Who shouted: Ginger, the gamekeeper, Peter, the gang, a stranger? Do not miss anyone.
9. Where was the gun pointing when it was fired?
10. Explain: running full-pelt, rustling, movement, underfoot, a wood-pigeon, breathless, treetops, disappeared, warren, keeper, gang.

B 1. What suggests that this happened at night?
2. Who do you think Ginger was?
3. What do you think the gang was doing?
4. Why was Peter not with the gang?
5. (a) Why did Peter not shout immediately? (b) What would *you* have done?
6. Which adjective describes Peter: resolute, skilful, nervous, cunning, bold?
7. (a) What does *caught out* mean? (b) How was Peter caught out?
8. What was the mysterious noise in the wood and what caused it?
9. (a) Say why the word "Keeper" is written like this: "Kee—per!"
   (b) Say when someone might say the same word like this: (i) "Keeper." or (ii) "Keeper?" or (iii) "Keeper!"
10. What is the meaning of: in one vast ache to hear, like the patter of rain blown out of the treetops, the thump of a rabbit, Peter's heart froze into a tiny screwed-up ball and died, headed towards; Listening to one, deaf to another; cupped his hands, a rush of shot, in the direction of, a chance intruder?

7 *Ships of War*

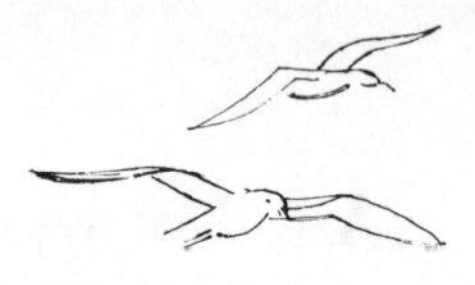

At Flores in the Azores Sir Richard Grenville lay,
And a pinnace, like a fluttered bird, came flying from far away:
"Spanish ships of war at sea; we have sighted fifty-three!"
Then sware Lord Thomas Howard: " 'Fore God I am no coward;
But I cannot meet them here, for my ships are out of gear,
And the half my men are sick. I must fly, but follow quick.
We are six ships of the line; can we fight with fifty-three?"

Then spake Sir Richard Grenville: "I know you are no coward;
You fly them for a moment to fight with them again.
But I've ninety men and more that are lying sick ashore.
I should count myself the coward if I left them, my Lord Howard,
To these Inquisition dogs and the devildoms of Spain."

So Lord Howard past away with five ships of war that day,
Till he melted like a cloud in the silent summer heaven;
But Sir Richard bore in hand all his sick men from the land
Very carefully and slow,
Men of Bideford in Devon,
And we laid them on the ballast down below;
For we brought them all aboard,
And they blest him in their pain, that they were not left to Spain,
To the thumbscrew and the stake.

From *The Revenge* by Lord Tennyson

Comprehension

A 1. Where did this take place?
2. (a) Give the names of two famous Elizabethan sailors, from this extract.
(b) Give the name of another, if you can.
3. How many enemy ships were coming?
4. To which country did the enemy ships belong?
5. What happened to the English ships?
6. Why could Lord Howard not fight the enemy?
7. Why did the sailors bless Sir Richard Grenville?
8. What was the home-town of the English sailors?
9. (a) Where were the sick men placed? (b) Can you think why they were put there?
10. What do these words mean: sighted, coward, melted, aboard?

B 1. (a) What do you think a pinnace is? (b) Why did it come?
2. (a) What are ships of the line: ships out of gear, liners, warships, pinnaces?
(b) What tells us that Grenville's ship, the *Revenge*, was a "ship of the line"?
3. Who was Lord Thomas Howard? Clues in the poem-extract will help you.
4. Why did Sir Richard refuse to leave his sick men behind?
5. Why are we not surprised to know that his men came from Devon?
6. (a) If one man is attacked by three, the fight is *three to one*.
When the "Revenge" stayed to fight the whole Spanish fleet, it was . . . .
(b) Such a fight was (frequent, hopeful, heroic but hopeless, fair). Which?
7. Choose an approximate date for this battle: 1066, 1492, 1600, 1900.
8. (a) Lord Howard was (brave, rash, cowardly, sensible). Which?
(b) Sir Richard was (thoughtless, kind-hearted, lying, enraged). Which?
9. Which meaning fits the end of the extract? (The enemy would be kind. Prisoners would be tortured and killed. The Spaniards would leave them behind.)
10. What is the meaning of: like a fluttered bird, came flying, meet them, out of gear, fly them for a moment, melted like a cloud, bore in hand, ballast, Sir Richard Grenville lay?

7 Language

1. Change the verbs to the Present tense:

   I am (carry) he (carry) it (crash) it is (die) they are (win) it (dry).

2. COLLECTIVE NOUNS The Spanish *fleet* attacked the "Revenge".

   We call a collection or group of ships a *fleet*: the Spanish fleet, a fishing fleet, a fleet of ships.

   Complete these collections: a —— of cards, a —— of loaves or bread, a —— of newspapers, sticks or rags, a clump of ——, a flock of —— (several), a herd of —— (several), a shoal of ——, a pack of —— (several), a school of ——.

   Remember: (1) Names of collections or groups are called Collective nouns.

   (2) Collective nouns are usually singular:

   The Spanish *fleet* of fifty-three warships IS sailing towards us.

   The whole *school* IS proud of you.

   BUT some collective nouns are regarded as plural:

   The *congregation* stood up and opened THEIR hymn books.

3. *Find the Stranger* Bideford Devon London Spaniards Yorkshire

4. Use in sentences: courage, courageous, courageously, encourage.

   Say what part of speech each of those four words is.

5. Give the meaning of these abbreviations: I've, you'll, o'er, he'd, don't, doesn't, we've, they're, can't, shan't, won't, it's.

6. Use in sentences: its, it's.

7. Think of words which sound exactly the same but which are spelt differently: pain, sighted, stake, so, bore, their, crews, current, cygnet, cymbals. Give the meaning of your words; also of the last three in the list.

8. Which words in the Comprehension poem rhyme with Spain, Heaven, ashore, Howard, hand?

   Which of these words rhymes with SEAS: see, maze, reasons, siege, freeze?

9. Put into alphabetical order: careful, silent, can, follow, summer, coward, cow

10. *Spelling* (a) and (b) two noises: squ...... and squ...... (c) men, women and children: p...... (d) to think it: bel.... (e) Thieves, etc. are often taken to a pol...-sta.... (f) cannot be seen: inv...... (g) vanish: dis...... (h) upset when something did not happen: dis......... (i) full of mystery: m......ous (j) an unexpected event: s....ise.

11. Write correctly these two sentences which were spoken when two friends met:
  May I come with you John asked David.
  No shouted David turning to go alone.
12. Make the second pair agree in the same way that the first pair agree:

badger, set	:	mole, ——
thirty, sixty	:	ten, ——
sun, sunshine	:	moon, ——
field, grass	:	forest, ——
former, latter	:	ancient, ——
shepherd, sheep	:	nurse, ——
natural, unnatural	:	legible, ——
mountain, summit	:	wave, ——

13. Rewrite this, making it more descriptive through the use of *vivid* adjectives:
  The very loud thunder, the very bright flashes of lightning and our dangerous position made us wish we had not left our nice shelter. As the bad weather became rapidly worse, we became very frightened.
14. Say which ONE of these sentences is correct and what is wrong with the others:
  (i) The climber thought he'd never reach the summit.
  (ii) The monitor hasn't rung the bell.
  (iii) "The monitor hasn't rung the bell yet," said the teacher.
  (iv) Fortunately the ship wasn't damaged.
15. The poems in Exercises 2 and 7 (Comprehension) are *narrative poems*. Why?
16. Use in five sentences: half my men silent summer heaven five ships all aboard revenge.

Find Out

1. Find what these words mean, then use one from each group in sentences:
  coward, cowardly, cowardice, cowherd, cowed, cower, cowl, cowslip, cowboy, cowrie board, bored, bore, boar, broad florist, floral, florin, flour, flourish pinnace, pinnacle, pineapple, pinion, pioneer, pinafore, pine, pinch, pincers.
2. Find the meaning of: under someone's thumb, thumb a lift, Tom Thumb, Thumbelina, thumb-prints, thumb-marks, thumbs up (also its origin or where it came from); half the battle, too clever by half, half-hearted, half measures, six of one and half a dozen of the other, Half a loaf is better than no bread.

3. *Corrections* "I must fly but follow quick." Follow *quickly* (adverb).
   Find eight more examples of poetic or out of date spelling or grammar in the extract from *The Revenge* and say what we should write nowadays.
4. *Elizabethan Sea-dogs* Find out about the sailors of Elizabeth I's reign, 400 years ago: Drake, Hawkins, Frobisher, Howard, Grenville, etc.

   Who or what were these: the Armada, fire-ships, El Draco, the Pelican, the Golden Hind, Sir Thomas Doughty, a famous game of bowls, One Against Fifty-three?

   What is the connection between Drake's ship and a cricket-pitch?

List of Poems

The Revenge by Tennyson.
The Armada by Macaulay.
The Spanish Armado (anonymous).
The Night of Trafalgar by Thomas Hardy.
A Ballad to Queen Elizabeth by Austin Dobson.
The Fighting Temeraire; The Old Superb; Drake's Drum by Sir Henry Newbolt.
Ye Mariners of England; Battle of the Baltic by Thomas Campbell.
The Old Navy by Frederick Marryat.

Comprehension comes at the end of this exercise.

8 *Language*

1. What collective nouns do we use for the following:
   sheep; cattle in a field; cattle being driven along a road; singers; bees, ants or insects; puppies, kittens, cubs or piglets; thieves; flowers; hay?
2. VERBS: PAST TENSE

Be careful with the Simple Past tense (like *I ran*) and the Past tense with "have, having, has or had" (like *I have run*).

Remember: (1) There are so many different ways of changing verbs from the Present tense to the Simple Past OR to the Past tense with "have, etc." that you must learn each verb separately.

You will find, however, that many verbs change like this:

(i) Simple Past: a   Past with "have", etc.: u

he ran, he has run she began, she has begun they drank, they have drunk

(ii) Past with "have", etc.: ends in N or EN

I had beaten it has bitten she has broken he has driven I have drawn

(2) The Past with "have, having, has or had" is also the Past with "am, is, are, was, were, be, been or being": it was broken, it has been forgotten, it is done.

Fill in the missing verbs:

Present Tense or Time	*Simple Past*	*Past with "have", etc.*
I spring	I sprang	I have sprung
The boats are sinking	The boats ——	The boats have——
Glass breaks easily	The glass —— easily	The glass was easily ——
He brings	He ——	He has ——
I swim every day	I —— every day	I have —— every day
She sings at concerts	She —— at concerts	She has —— at concerts

3. *Find the Stranger* practice dexterity accidents articles useful
4. Think of words which sound exactly the same but which are spelt differently:
   weather, idle, cause, dear, dew, die, doe, draught, dying, faint.

   Give the meaning of your words.
5. Think of words for stormy weather, like gale.
6. ". . . *practice* and dexterity compensated for want of strength."

   Remember: (1) practice: NOUN practise: VERB

There will be *a practice* tonight. We *must practise* tonight.

Some more c or s words: advice, advise; prophecy, prophesy; licence, license.

(2) c: noun s: verb c, n and s, v in alphabetical order

OR good *advice* (noun); Please *advise* me. (You can hear the difference.)

(3) The nouns may be singular or plural: many practices, one licence.

The verbs may be in any tense: practising, licensed, etc.

Put one of the words in the gap, changing the word-ending if necessary:

(i) practice, practise : —— hard if you wish to play well.

(ii) licence, license : How much does a dog- —— cost?

(iii) advice, advise : Good —— helps us all.

(iv) prophecy, prophesy : Joseph —— seven years of famine.

7. Which proverb fits the Comprehension extract, "Winter Work"?

(a) Too many cooks spoil the broth. (b) Practice makes perfect.

(c) A bad workman blames his tools. (d) New brooms sweep clean.

8. Put into alphabetical order: ever, England, Edward, Edith, every, each, evening.

9. *Spelling* (a) forefathers: an....... (b) a gathering of people: ass..... (c) They live in cities: cit..... (d) looking forward eagerly to a surprise: ex...ed (e) say what something looks like: give a d......tion (f) Ice makes roads sli..... (g) not satisfied: dis......... (h) and (i) the coming and going of trains: ar..... and dep...... (j) short: br...

10. Use in sentences: the noun from the verb *instruct*; the verb from the noun *destruction*; the adjective from the noun *strength*; the adverb from the verb *sweeten*.

11. Give words which mean the same as remained, idle, opportunity, instruct, damp, mishaps, lift, occurred, errors, several, little, mend, rapidly, happy.

12. Use *there*, *their*, *they're* in one sentence, in any order.

13. Say which words are correct: (i) (bought, brought) at a shop (ii) (Lie, Lay) down! (iii) go for something: (bring, fetch) (iv) (whose, who's) cap.

14. Form opposites by adding these prefixes: un, im, in, dis, ir, il: happy, contented, legal, direct, possible, wise, trust, regular, correct, sincere.

15. Write two sentences in Direct Speech, one person replying to the other's question.

16. Use in five sentences: in the evening not surprising carpenter's tools signs of impatience victory.

Find Out

1. Find what these words mean, then use one from each group in sentences:
   accident, incident, precedent, president, resident, residence   idle, idol
   interior, exterior, internal, external, entrance, exit, eternal
   property, properly, prophecy, proposition, proprietor   articles, particles.
2. Find the meaning of: have something at one's fingertips, put one's finger on the cause of the trouble, fingers all thumbs, fingerprints, light-fingered; as hard as nails, hit the nail on the head, pay on the nail, nail someone down; be out of the wood, unable to see the wood for the trees.
3. *Wood-words* Find the meaning of: wood (3), wood-pigeon, wood-lark, woodpecker, wood-leopard, woodman, woodsman, wood-wind, woodwork, woodbine, woodchuck, woodcock, woodcut, woodcutter, wooded, woodland, wood-pulp, wooden, woody.
4. *Forests* Make a list of forests from your atlas, saying where each one is.
   Find out what these have to do with forests: the Rufus Stone, Verderers, Royal Forests, Lyndhurst, Sir Walter Tyrrell, the Grand Avenue, Robin Hood, Anderida, Waltham, Major Oak.

Book List

The Children of the New Forest by Captain Marryat.
Simon; The Shield Ring; Warrior Scarlet; Outcast by Rosemary Sutcliff.
The Trumpet and the Swan by Marjorie Bowen.
The Gauntlet; Knight Crusader by Ronald Welch.
Three Golden Nobles by Christine Price.
The Wool-Pack; Load of Unicorn; Ring Out Bow Bells by Cynthia Harnett.
Redcap Runs Away by Rhoda Power.
Adam of the Road by Elizabeth J. Gray.
The Noble Hawks by Ursula M. Williams.
A Child's Day Through the Ages by Dorothy M. Stuart.
The Namesake; The Marsh King by C. W. Hodges.
The Last of the Vikings by Henry Treece.

8 *Winter Work*

But if they remained indoors during the inclement weather they were not idle. Jacob took this opportunity to instruct the children in everything. Alice learnt how to wash and how to cook. It is true that sometimes she scalded herself a little, sometimes she burnt her fingers; and other accidents did occur, from the articles employed being too heavy for them to lift by themselves; but practice and dexterity compensated for want of strength, and fewer accidents happened every day. Humphrey had his carpenter's tools; and although at first he had many failures, and wasted nails and wood, by degrees he learnt to use his tools with more dexterity, and made several little useful articles. Little Edith could now do something, for she made and baked all the oatmeal cakes, which saved Alice a good deal of time and trouble in watching them.

In the evening Alice sat down with her needle and thread to mend the clothes. At first they were not very well done; but she improved every day. Edith and Humphrey learnt to read while Alice worked, and then Alice learnt; and thus passed the winter away so rapidly, that, although they had been five months at the cottage, it did not appear as if they had been there as many weeks. All were happy and contented, with the exception, perhaps, of Edward, who had fits of gloominess, and occasionally showed signs of impatience as to what was passing in the world, of which he remained in ignorance.

That Edward Beverley had fits of gloominess and impatience is not surprising. He was not two miles from that property which by right was his own. He sighed for the time when the king's cause should be again triumphant, and his arrival at that age when he could in person support and uphold the cause. He longed to be in command as his father had been—to lead his men on to victory—to recover his property, and to revenge himself on those who had acted so cruelly towards him.

From *The Children of the New Forest* by Captain Marryat

Comprehension

This story is set in the Civil War in England, over 300 years ago, when King Charles I and his Cavaliers fought against the Parliamentary troops under Oliver Cromwell.

A 1. Were the children lazy or industrious?

2. Who was their teacher?

3. Why did he teach them? (They asked him to teach them. They were sent to him to be taught. It helped to pass away the long winter. He was a schoolmaster.)

4. What were the children's Christian names (forenames)?

5. Why did accidents happen?

6. Complete this sentence:
The children were living with —— in a —— in the —— ——.

7. (a) Who was unhappy? (b) Why?

8. How long had the children been at the cottage?

9. In which season of the year did they stay indoors?

10. What is the meaning of: indoors, scalded, many failures, improved, contented, gloominess, victory, revenge?

B 1. What is inclement weather, according to the clues in the extract?

2. What was Alice's surname? The children are all from the same family.

3. (a) Whom did Edward support in the Civil War: Cavaliers or Roundheads?
(b) What tells us?

4. What suggests that the Roundheads were winning?

5. Why did Edward wish he were older?

6. (a) What do you think his father had been?
(b) How can we tell that he was dead?

7. (a) How far were the children from their real home?
(b) How can we tell that they had been turned out of it?

8. Why do you think they had been turned out of their home?

9. (a) Who was the eldest child? (b) How do you know?

10. What is the meaning of: opportunity, the articles employed, practice, dexterity, compensated for want of strength, by degrees, fits of gloominess, signs of impatience, what was passing in the world, remained in ignorance, property, the king's cause, triumphant, support and uphold the cause?

9 *There She Blows!*

I stood gazing up at the clouds whence that voice dropped like a wing. High aloft in the cross-trees was that mad Gay-Header, Tashtego. His body was reaching eagerly forward, his hand stretched out like a wand, and at brief sudden intervals he continued his cries. To be sure that same sound was that very moment perhaps being heard all over the seas, from hundreds of whalemen's look-outs perched as high in the air; but from few of those lungs could that accustomed old cry have derived such a marvellous cadence as from Tashtego the Indian's.

As he stood hovering over you half suspended in air, so wildly and eagerly peering towards the horizon, you would have thought him some prophet or seer beholding the shadows of Fate, and by those wild cries announcing their coming.

"There she blows! There! There! There! She blows! She blows!"

"Where-away?"

"On the lee-beam, about two miles off! A school of them!"

Instantly all was commotion.

The sperm-whale blows as a clock ticks, with the same undeviating and reliable uniformity. And thereby whalemen distinguish this fish from other tribes of his genus.

"There go flukes!" was now the cry from Tashtego; and the whales disappeared.

"Quick, steward!" cried Ahab. "Time! Time!"

Dough-boy hurried below, glanced at the watch, and reported the exact minute to Ahab.

From *Moby Dick* by Herman Melville

Comprehension

A 1. Who shouted "There she blows!"?
2. Why did he shout this?
3. Did the look-out shout once, twice or often?
4. (a) Did he see any shadows? (b) How do you know?
5. How far away were the whales?
6. (a) What was the steward's name? (b) What do you think was his work?
7. (a) Did someone have a ticking clock? (b) How do you know?
8. What happened to the whales, in this extract?
9. Why did the look-out say "On the lee-beam"?
10. Explain: gazing up, a wand, continued his cries, look-outs, eagerly, hovering, announcing.

B 1. How did these sailors earn their living?
2. (a) Think of at least three adjectives to describe the man *you* would choose as look-out.
(b) Explain why you would choose such a man.
3. Who do you think Ahab was?
4. ". . . . whalemen distinguish *this fish*. . . ." What would *you* call it?
5. (a) What do you think the whales' flukes are? (b) Why do you think so?
6. How can a sperm-whale be recognised?
7. Write in your own words: (a) Instantly all was commotion. (b) at brief sudden intervals (c) you would have thought him (d) announcing their coming.
8. (a) What is a prophet or seer? (b) Who looked like one? (c) Why?
9. Of which countries could Tashtego be a native?
10. What is the meaning of: cross-trees, that mad Gay-Header, accustomed old cry, have derived such a marvellous cadence, half suspended in air, the horizon, beholding the shadows of Fate, the lee-beam, a school of them, the same undeviating and reliable uniformity, distinguish this fish from other tribes of his genus (kind or type), commotion?

9 Language

1. Make two columns: *Simple Past* *Past with "have", etc.*

   ran have run

   Change these verbs to the correct spelling to fit the two columns:

   draw, drive, eat, fall, bite, come.

2. VERBS: FUTURE TENSE

   The Future tense presents difficulties in the use of *will* or *shall*.

   The simplest fact to remember is that we usually say this:

   I shall, we shall he will, you will, they will

   If we use *the other word*: I will, we will; he shall, you shall, they shall; we change the meaning and show *determination*:

   I *will* win this race! (I am determined to win!)

   They *shall* not pass! (They must not be allowed to pass!)

   Remember: I shall, we shall; he will, you will, they will: simple statements.

   I *will*, we *will*; he *shall*, you *shall*, they *shall*: determination!

   Say what the difference in meaning is here:

   (i) I shall not be late tonight.

   (ii) I will not be late tonight!

   Say which word, *will* or *shall*, goes into each space:

   (i) He —— try to arrive early.

   (ii) We —— not be long.

   (iii) I —— climb this hill, even if it takes all day!

   (iv) Fight on! We —— not be beaten!

3. *Find the Stranger* gazing sound commotion cries noise
4. Think of words of similar meaning: continued, cries, gazing, dropped, aloft, stretch out, accustomed, marvellous, behold, the coming of.
5. Think of opposites: forward, brief, sudden, continued, same, wildly, eagerly, arrive, commotion, reliable.
6. Write correctly:

   the old indian tashtego that gay friendly seafarer reached eagerly forward pointing to the whales there she blows he shouted there she blows

7. Put into Indirect Speech:

   "There she blows!" yelled Tashtego. "A whole school of whales!"

8. Say which of these words are nouns and which are verbs; then change nouns to

verbs and verbs to nouns (like this:

the blaze: noun; verb: to blaze hesitate: verb; noun: hesitation):

growth, invent, objection, injure, disappear, courage, provision, relief.

9. Use these conjunctions (joining-words) in sentences:

because, until, before, unless, but.

10. Put into alphabetical order: marvellous, cadence, lungs, cries, there, like, whales, look-out, lee-beam, announcing, mad.

11. What word should be in the place of the wrong one in each sentence?

(i) Do not forget to distinguish the light before you leave.

(ii) The prisoners' uniformity was a drab, shapeless suit.

(iii) The unhappy budgerigar draped on its perch.

(iv) The look-out was black for the starving people in the besieged city.

(v) The exciting news was soon overall the town.

12. What is the plural of: voice, body, cry, whale, fish, valley, hero, son, claw, lady, gentleman, day, buoy, ox, salmon?

13. *Spelling* (a) famous but bad: not . . . . . . (b) confused and uncomfortable: emb . . . . (c) sticking out: prot . . . . . . (d) a musical beat: r . . th . (e) not weakness: str . . . . . (f) chance: opp . . . . (g) not done on purpose: acc . . . . ly (h) went on, forward: pro . . . . . . (i) went on in front: pre . . . . . (j) went back: rec . . . .

14. What is the difference between a horde and a tribe of savages; a cloud and a swarm of insects; a crowd, a mob, an assembly, an audience, a queue, a group of people?

15. What do we call people who (i) work in coal-mines (ii) sell tea, sugar and bacon (iii) sell vegetables (iv) look after schools, offices, etc. (v) build (vi) play football (vii) conduct (viii) govern (ix) tour (x) look after sheep?

16. What is an adverb? Write a sentence containing one, underlining the adverb.

17. Use in five sentences: hovering high aloft the horizon the whales disappeared "Quick, steward!"

Find Out

1. Find what these words mean, then use one from each group in sentences:

aboard, a board, broad, abroad, breadth whales, Wales, weals, wheels

seize, siege, besiege, sieve accustomed, accumulate, accurate

derive, deride, deprive, contrive, pride, stride suspend, suspect, prospect.

2. Find the meaning of: cry for the moon, cry off, cry over spilt milk, much cry and little wool, war-cry, battle-cry, in full cry, a far cry, cry-baby, cry down, cry quits, town crier.
3. *Collective Nouns* Find out unusual ones, like a gaggle of geese.
   What are these collective nouns: a pride, building, wisp, plague, muster, skein, troop, murmuration, covey, convoy, string, skulk?
4. *Whaling* Find out about whales and whaling: the different kinds of whales; where and how they are caught.
   What are these: sea-canaries, sea-unicorns, blubber, factory ships, baleen, cachalots, narwhals, spermaceti, ambergris, close season?

Book List

Moby Dick by Herman Melville.
Danger to Windward by Armstrong Sperry.
The Cruise of the Cachalot by F. T. Bullen.
About Whales by Allan Moore.
The Adventure of Whaling by Frank Crisp.
Arctic Whaling Adventures by Michael Hyde.
Deep-Sea Fishing by John M. Wright.
The Deep-Sea Fisherman by I. E. Allison.
Adventure of the Sea by James Fisher.
Discovering Deep-Sea Fishing by Roy Perrott.
Whale's Way by Joanna Johnston.
My Boy John That Went to Sea by James V. Marshall.

Comprehension comes at the end of this exercise.

10 *Language*

1. (a) Say what these two sentences mean:
   (i) We shall not come. (ii) We will not come!
   (b) Use the correct word:
   I think I (will, shall) be allowed to stay up late.
2. ADVERBS What is an adverb? What is a common ending of adverbs?
   To what do we add that common ending?
   Write down six adverbs and say from which adjectives they come.
   There are several kinds of adverbs but the most common are those which tell us HOW something was done:
   The small boy ran *quickly*. HOW he ran: quickly.
   Two more kinds of adverbs: (1) He began to whistle, looking *everywhere*.
   The adverb *everywhere* tells us WHERE he was looking.
   (2) He began to whistle but *soon* stopped.
   The adverb *soon* tells us WHEN he stopped.
   Remember: Adverbs which tell us HOW the action was done are Adverbs of Manner.
   Adverbs which tell us WHERE the action was done: Adverbs of Place.
   Adverbs which tell us WHEN the action was done: Adverbs of Time.
   Pick out the adverbs and say which kind they are:
   (i) Something was moving ahead. (ii) Please come soon. (iii) You may stay now. (iv) Something was moving stealthily. (v) Please come quietly. (vi) You may stay there.
3. *Find the Stranger* shower sower better border
4. What are ALL the meanings of stand, fly, sweeps, lie, loose, steer, blow, till, ground, spring?
5. What can we call all the things on each line (e.g. fox, lion, badger: *wild animals*; quickly, slowly, carefully: *adverbs*)?
   redden, ask, let, fling, give
   maple, sun, plough, voice, sea
   generous, faithful, grateful, glad, gay
   green, white, black, crimson, scarlet
   builder, clerk, nurse, carpenter, salesman

'twixt, I've, phone, pram, Hants.

: ! ? . , ;

seize, freeze, please, knees, keys.

6. Think of words which sound exactly the same but which are spelt differently: sun, beech, border, whose, him, where, gilds, sea, hear.
Give the meaning of your words.
7. *Spelling* (a) break into a conversation: int..... (b) enough: suf....... (c) flowing water: cur.... (d) a fruit: cur.... (e) not often: occ.......ly (f) often: fre.....ly (g) again and again: rep.....ly (h) upset; worried: agi..... (i) make fresh: fr..... (j) carrot: veg.....
8. Use *past* and *passed* in two sentences.
9. Change to the Past tense with "have", like break, *have broken*: redden in the sun, beeches stand, gay leaves fly, sweeps the sky, dark acres furrowed lie, we give, they ask.
10. Give the opposite of distant, generous, shining, gay, fresh, dark, ask, tired, sleeping, clatter.
11. Give words of similar meaning to the words in Question 10.
12. (a) Which words in the poem rhyme with stand, lie, ground, gale, grow?
(b) Which of these words rhymes with HOARSE: oar, art, force, grass?
13. (a) What is the difference between these collections or groups: a rabble, throng, multitude, congregation, crowd?
(b) What are these groups: spectators, witnesses, bystanders, staff, a jury, a team?
14. Use in two sentences: its, it's.
15. What is a pronoun? Give five examples.
16. Use in sentences: redden in the sun autumn gold golden shower emerald blades in the willowy vale.

Find Out

1. Find what these words mean, then use one from each group in sentences:
redden, deaden, leaden tired, tried, attired, retired, tires, tyres
plough, dough, rough, cough, thorough, through acres, aches
grange, range, strange, orange, arrange, disarrange, rearrange
assemble, reassemble, resemble loose, lose, loss, lost.
2. Find the meaning of: steer clear of trouble, danger, etc., a rabbit punch,

act the goat, the lion's share, beard the lion in his den, lion-hearted, foxy, fox someone, foxgloves, fox-terriers, hound someone, ride to hounds, like a bull in a china-shop, a cock and bull story, like a bull at a gate, John Bull, a bull's-eye, bull-terrier, bulldog, bullfight, bullfinch, March comes in like a lion and goes out like a lamb.

3. *Animal Families* Make a list (Father, Mother, Young; also, if possible, Home and Collective noun), especially of unusual family words like this:
   swans: cob, pen, cygnet, etc.
4. *Poetry* (a) Make up a poem about one of the seasons of the year.
   (b) Find a poem for each of the following groups (like this: *animals*: "The Squirrel" by Mary Howitt): the seasons (four poems), mountains, work, weather, battles, the sea, travel, animals, children, birds, famous rides, night, streams, smugglers or highwaymen, railways, cities, the countryside.

List of Poems

The Song of the Sower by William Cullen Bryant.
Seasons; Summer; A Year's Windfalls by Christina Rossetti.
Child's Song in Spring; Summer Song by E. Nesbit.
First Spring Morning; North Wind in October by Robert Bridges.
Autumn by F. Politzer.
February by Francis Brett Young.
The Coming of Spring; Birds in Summer by Mary Howitt.
To Daffodils by Robert Herrick.
October by Robert Frost.
Home Thoughts from Abroad by Robert Browning.

10

The Sower's Song

The maples redden in the sun;
  In autumn gold the beeches stand;
Rest, faithful plough, thy work is done
  Upon the teeming land.
Bordered with trees whose gay leaves fly
On every breath that sweeps the sky,
The fresh dark acres furrowed lie,
  And ask the sower's hand.
Loose the tired steer and let him go
To pasture where the gentians blow,
And we, who till the grateful ground,
Fling we the golden shower around.

Fling wide the generous grain; we fling
O'er the dark mould the green of spring.
For thick the emerald blades shall grow,
When first the March winds melt the snow,
And to the sleeping flowers, below,
  The early bluebirds sing.
Fling wide the grain; we give the fields
  The ears that nod in summer's gale,
The shining stems that summer gilds,
  The harvest that o'erflows the vale,
And swells, an amber sea, between
The full-leaved woods, its shores of green.

From *The Song of the Sower* by William Cullen Bryant

Comprehension

A 1. What are (a) red (b) golden? Why?
2. In which season is the sower singing his song?
3. How can a plough be "faithful"?
4. How are the leaves gay?
5. What do you think *gentians* are?
6. (a) What is "the golden shower": rain, sunshine, seed or gold?
   (b) Why is this a clever description?
7. When will the green shoots appear?
8. What are the *ears* and *shining stems* in the second verse?
9. Why are the flowers asleep?
10. What is the meaning of: maples, redden, beeches, bordered with trees, furrowed, let him go to pasture, the ears that nod, o'erflows the vale?

B 1. (a) What breath "sweeps the sky"? (b) What does it do?
2. (a) What is a steer? (b) Why is it weary?
3. "And ask the sower's hand." What does this mean?
4. How can the earth be *grateful*?
5. (a) What is the *amber sea*? (b) Why is it called this?
6. How can the autumn sower "fling . . . the green of spring"?
7. (a) What are *early* bluebirds?
   (b) When are they first heard?
   (c) Why do *you* think they sing?
8. Explain the last six lines of the second verse.
9. Make a list of words or phrases in the poem which suggest that this song is not about sowing in our own country. Explain why each one suggests this.
10. What is the meaning of: autumn gold, thy work is done, the teeming land, till the ground, generous grain, dark mould, emerald blades, summer gilds, the full-leaved woods?

11 A Peaceful Scene

"Ah!" said Good, surveying these shining-leaved trees with evident enthusiasm, "here is plenty of wood. Let us stop and cook some dinner; I have about digested that raw meat."

Nobody objected to this, so leaving the road we made our way to a stream which was babbling away not far away, and soon had a goodly fire of dry boughs blazing. Cutting off some substantial hunks from the flesh of the *inco* which we had brought with us we proceeded to toast them on the end of sharp sticks, as one sees the Kafirs do, and ate them with relish. After filling ourselves, we lit our pipes and gave ourselves up to enjoyment, which, compared with the hardships we had recently undergone, seemed almost heavenly.

The brook, of which the banks were clothed with dense masses of a gigantic species of maiden-hair fern interspersed with feathery tufts of wild asparagus, babbled merrily at our side, the soft air murmured through the leaves of the silver trees, doves cooed around, and bright-winged birds flashed like living gems from bough to bough. It was a Paradise.

The magic of the place combined with an overwhelming sense of dangers left behind, and of the Promised Land reached at last, seemed to charm us into silence. Sir Henry and Umbopa sat conversing in a mixture of broken English and kitchen Zulu in a low voice, but earnestly enough, and I lay, with my eyes half shut, upon that fragrant bed of fern and watched them.

From *King Solomon's Mines* by H. Rider Haggard

Comprehension

A 1. (a) Where was a fire made? (b) What is a *goodly* fire?
2. Why do you think they made their fire near a stream?
3. How did they cook the meat?
4. Whose way of cooking was this?
5. What did they do after the meal?
6. What grew on the banks of the stream?
7. (a) What looked like jewels? (b) Why?
8. Who sat talking?
9. Why was the place a Paradise?
10. What is the meaning of: objected, boughs, hunks, proceeded, toast, hardships, dense masses, doves, cooed, bright-winged, conversing, mixture, fragrant bed?

B 1. (a) Why was the man Good pleased? (b) Why was he eager to cook dinner?
2. "Nobody objected to this." To what?
3. (a) To which African tribe did Umbopa probably belong? (b) What suggests this?
4. Which trees in our own country are silver?
5. How do you know that these men had not had an easy time?
6. What magic was there in that place?
7. (a) Can you guess or work out the meaning of "broken English and kitchen Zulu"? (b) Why *kitchen* Zulu?
8. One word tells us that these men were not travelling through the middle of a trackless jungle. Which word is it?
9. Name all noises, loud or soft, which broke the silence of that place.
10. What is the meaning of: surveying, with evident enthusiasm, substantial hunks, inco, Kafirs, with relish, gave ourselves up to enjoyment, the banks were clothed, a gigantic species, interspersed with feathery tufts, flashed like living gems, an overwhelming sense, earnestly enough, the Promised Land?

11 Language

1. Insert suitable adverbs:

   Nobody objected —— to this, so we —— made our way to a nearby stream which was babbling —— and —— had a cheerful fire of dry boughs blazing ——.

2. PRONOUNS What is a pronoun? "Pro" means "in place of".

   There are several different kinds of pronouns with difficult names like demonstrative pronouns, etc. Try to remember as many actual pronouns as you can: I, you, he, she, it, we, they, me, him, her, my, who, which, etc.

   Using pronouns in place of nouns enables us to avoid repeating the same nouns over and over again. Here are parts of the Comprehension extract without pronouns:

   Cutting off some substantial hunks . . . we proceeded to toast the substantial hunks . . . and ate the substantial hunks with relish.

   Using pronouns, it becomes:

   Cutting off some substantial hunks . . . we proceeded to toast *them* . . . and ate *them* with relish.

   Use pronouns to avoid repetition of nouns:

   (i) Sir Henry and Sir Henry's friends. (ii) Good said, "Good has digested the raw meat." (iii) The explorers lit the pipes belonging to the explorers and gave the explorers up to enjoyment. (iv) One man lay, with one man's eyes half-shut.

   Remember: (1) The pronoun WHO refers to people.
   The pronoun WHICH refers to creatures and things.
   We met a man who . . . with a dog which . . .

   (2) Many people make mistakes when they use pronouns. Which are correct in the following sentences?

   (a) (Me and John, I and John, John and I) went to the fair.
   (b) The reward was given to (me and Tony, Tony and I, Tony and me, I and Tony).
   (c) Let (me and you, you and I, you and me) go together.
   (d) Between (you and me, you and I), it is easy to see who did it.
   (e) (Who, Whom) did you hit?
   (f) These are the books (which, who, what) I like best of all.

3. *Find the Stranger* stream boughs sticks pipes trees

4. ". . . we proceeded to toast them."
   What do these words (verbs) mean: proceed, precede, recede?
   Use one of the verbs in a sentence.
5. borrow, lend.
   Remember: When you ask for the pencil-sharpener, you wish to borrow it. The person who owns it will lend it to you.
   Always say "Please may *I borrow* it?" or "Please will *you lend* it to me?"
   Correct, if wrong, remembering that *the owner lends* something:
   (i) I tried to lend a rubber but nobody had one.
   (ii) I will lend you my pencil if you wish to borrow it.
6. *Spelling* (a) strong: pow..... (b) not enough: insuf....... (c) trouble or sorrow: dis..... (d) slid: slit..... (e) very old: anc.... (f) recalled to mind: rem....... (g) slowly: gra...... (h) sweet smell: fra...... (i) ended: ce.... (j) right through: thr.......
7. What are ALL the meanings of: sticks, crane, horse, relish, fearful, wood, object, stream, toast, pipes?
8. ". . . from bough to bough".
   Put these words in pairs according to their sound: bough, cough, rough, trough, dough, plough, though, borough, tough, thorough.
9. Say what parts of speech these words are: merrily, silence, mixture, babbled, leaving, gigantic, I, raw, dry, ate.
10. Put these in order, the smallest first: brook, spring, ocean, river, sea.
11. ". . . the flesh of the inco . . . ."
    What do we call the flesh or meat which we eat from pigs (3), cattle, sheep, calves, deer?
12. Think of words which sound exactly the same but which are spelt differently: made, boughs, ate, hair, fir, flew, flower, for, fourth, foul.
    Give the meaning of your words.
13. ". . . a stream which was babbling . . . the soft air murmured . . . doves cooed . . ."
    Think of verbs of sound to fit these nouns: donkey, lion, bull, (watchful) dog, (injured) dog, frog, lamb, hen, snake, owl, whip, door, steam, rapids.
14. Put into alphabetical order: road, raw, relish, reach, sat, silence, rider.
15. Put in prepositions: Sir Henry and Umbopa sat —— the grass, talking —— low voices —— the dangers —— the past few days. I sat —— a tree and listened —— them.

16. Use in sentences: dry boughs sharp sticks feathery tufts
like living gems magic fragrant bed of fern.

Find Out

1. Find what these words mean, then use one from each group in sentences:
   cataract, catalogue, catastrophe, catarrh babble, gabble, dabble, rabble
   survey, surveyor, survivor, suspicion paradise, parable, parachute, parallel
   undergo, undertake, underground, undergrowth, underhand, underline, undermine.
2. Find the meaning of: side with someone, a side-line, offside, sideboard, side-show, side-track; born with a silver spoon in the mouth, silver-tongued, silver wedding, silver birch, Every cloud has a silver lining.
3. *Streams* Make a list of nouns about water, like stream, tributary and straits. Give their meaning.
4. *Africa* Find out the names of the large countries in Africa and the answers to the following question: What are these: the Zambesi, Sahara, Kalahari, Victoria Falls, zebras, giraffes, ostriches, the Cape of Good Hope, veldt, wadis, oases, nomads, Suez Canal?

Book List

King Solomon's Mines by H. Rider Haggard.
Sirga; Sama; Elephant Road by René Guillot.
Shifta!; Ambari! by R. Forbes-Watson.
The Mamba's Precipice by Roy Campbell.
African Boy by Grace Huxtable.
The South African Twins by Daphne Rooke.
I, Mungo Park by Ronald Syme.
Lion of Africa: Livingstone by P. Pringle.
Opening Africa by L. F. Hobley.
Wagons Rolling North by W. Robertson.
A Zebra Came to Drink by Arthur Catherall.
The Bushbabies by William Stevenson.

Comprehension comes at the end of this exercise.

12

Language

1. Say which word you choose from those in the brackets:
   (i) This is the woman (what, which, that, who) saw the accident.
   (ii) The dog (who, what, that, which) stole the meat was starving.
   (iii) "(Its, It's) not very often that a fox will let you come close to (its, it's) cubs," said the old gamekeeper.
   (iv) David is not as old as (me, I).

2. PREPOSITIONS Words like *of*, *to*, *from*, *under*, *by*, *with*, *at*, *on* are called prepositions because they are "*pre-positioned*" or *placed in front of* words to complete the meaning, like this:

   He came *into* the room. I will come *with* you.

   Remember: different from
   full of; filled with
   interfere with, be angry with someone
   guilty of, die of, ashamed of, complain of, out of
   suffer from, rely on, similar to, aim at
   agree with someone, agree to something (like a plan, or agree to do something)
   change something for something else, change places with someone

   Insert the correct preposition in these sentences:
   (i) According —— my diary you should have gone on the 12th.
   (ii) We all aim —— a target of £500.
   (iii) Do not blame me —— your own mistake.
   (iv) He was not conscious —— the cold.
   (v) I disagree —— you.
   (vi) In June, 1944, the invasion —— Normandy took place.
   (vii) I will write —— my holiday spent —— friends and send it —— a magazine.

3. *Find the Stranger* swimming felt fought struggled

4. Put into alphabetical order: splash, water, surges, went, sizzle, surface, strokes, shocking, whirlpool, shot, sucked, want, air, distance.

5. Write these sentences correctly:
   (i) "He (don't, doesn't) know the answer," she said.

(ii) "I can't run (any, no) more," I gasped breathlessly.
(iii) He (done, did) all that damage.
(iv) The boy did not take (no, any) notice of my warning.
(v) "You must (of, have) seen the notice," said the teacher.
(vi) There (was, were) three knives on the table.

6. *Spelling* (a) used to something: acc....... (b) very big: gig..... (c) a talk or chat: con......... (d) a low muttering: m.r...... (e) dainty, not strong: del..... (f) a doctor: ph.....an (g) very ugly: hid.... (h) almost falling: tot...... (i) a chase: p.rs... (j) not bent: str.....
7. Change these verbs to the Simple Past tense, like RAN and the Past tense with "have", etc., like HAVE RUN: freeze, give, grow, ride, throw, write.
8. Add suitable adverbs (M: Manner, P: Place, T: Time) to these verbs and write short sentences: whistle (M) grope (P) come (T)
You may change the verbs to any tense.
9. Find in the Comprehension extract, "Splash!", four adjectives describing the sea, all in one short phrase.
10. Make sense out of these jumbled words:
ceased whirlpool foam the disappeared the and.
11. Complete this table, following the example of the first line:

ship	captain	crew	passengers	travel
school	——	——	——	——
hotel	——	——	——	——
bank	——	——	——	——

12. Write correctly:
(i) jennie peter called out hold on im coming
(ii) may i play with you john asked i promise to behave
(iii) no shouted peter angrily you promised yesterday then forgot your promise
13. (a) Think of verbs of sound for these: cats——, waves —— onto the beach, a ship's siren ——, a tap (dripping), a tap (turned on), a stream running among stones.
(b) What is the difference in meaning between these sounds of bare feet or shoes: tramp, patter, shuffling, a scuffle, squeaking, stamping, tapping, scraping, clatter?
14. Think of words which sound exactly the same but which are spelt differently: heels, fought, sea, saw, it's, faint, phrase, frees, gate, gamble.
Give the meaning of your words.

15. (a) Make three lists (nouns, adjectives, verbs) and put these words into the correct lists: *felt* something, do, the *grip*, whirlpool, the surface, green, full, depths, irresistible, he *shot*, a *gasp*, gasped, Countess, Jennie.
(b) Which parts of speech are these words: Peter, of, shockingly, she, and?
16. What is the (a) singular of thrusts, feet, legs, pianos, tomatoes, women?
(b) plural of cry, chimney, fairy, sheep, salmon, church?
17. Use in sentences: Splash! powerful strokes in the distance whirlpool a mouthful of salt water two vagrant cats.

Find Out

1. Find what these words mean, then use one from each group in sentences: revolving, revolting, reviving, revisiting, revising, reverting, reversing, revelling, revealing, reviling surface, service, surfeit thrust, thrush, trust, mistrust, distrust succeed, exceed, concede, precede.
2. Find the meaning of: not enough room to swing a cat, like a cat on hot bricks, let the cat out of the bag, raining cats and dogs, a cat and dog life, see which way the cat jumps, cat-calls, catapult, catering, caterpillar, catkins, catalogues, catastrophe, Care killed the cat. A cat may look at a king.
3. *Movement* 2 Make a list of verbs which tell us how animals, birds, etc. move, like this: Kangaroos leap. Lambs frisk or gambol.
4. *Seas and Oceans* Make a list of the seas and oceans of the world, beginning with the ones around Britain; also words connected with the sea.
What are these: fathoms, islets, peninsula, isthmus, headland, archipelago, atoll, buoys, reefs, shoals (2), wrecks, coastguards?

Book List

Jennie by Paul Gallico.
Mère Michel and her Cat by Margaret Cardew.
Sons of the Tiger by Patricia M. Case.
Smoky Joe by Laurence Meynell.
The Nine Lives of Island Mackenzie by Ursula M. Williams.
Sirga; Kpo the Leopard by René Guillot.
The Observer's Book of Cats by Grace Pond.
The Zoo Book by George Cansdale.

12 *Splash!*

Splash! Into the water Peter went!

It was roiling and boiling and full of sizzle and foam, surges, lifts, thrusts and undertows from the powerful strokes of the *Countess*' propeller just beneath the surface. Also it was shockingly cold.

Peter felt himself caught in the grip of an irresistible whirlpool; he was pulled down, rolled over, thrust head over heels, then shot to the surface, and before he could gasp his lungs full of air, sucked down again into the green depths. With his chest near to bursting from want of air, he fought and struggled to rise, swimming with all four feet, and at last reached the surface sufficiently far behind in the wake of the ship to be no longer subject to the forces stirred up by her machinery. The whirlpool died away, the choking white foam vanished, and he was swimming at last on top of the chill, salt, green and glassy sea.

Off in the distance, perhaps fifty or sixty yards away, he saw a tiny pinpoint of an object moving in the water and tried to call out—"Jennie! Don't be afraid! Hold out. It's me: Peter. I'm coming—" but succeeded in getting only a mouthful of salt water which tasted horrible, and thereafter he decided to keep his mouth closed and concentrate on reaching her side. But he thought he heard a faint answering cry from her, and finding that he had no difficulty in staying up now and holding his head out of the water by lifting his chin, he swam as rapidly as his four legs would take him in her direction.

What would happen when he reached her, he did not know, or at least he was not minded to think about, since it was certain that the sailor was quite right and the last thing Captain Sourlies would do was put the *Countess* about and stop her, losing precious time for no better purpose than to snatch two vagrant cats, who were aboard quite uninvited, at that, from a watery grave.

From *Jennie* by Paul Gallico

Comprehension

A 1. Peter and Jennie were (two children, brother and sister, two cats, two people). Which?

2. Peter fell into (a river, rapids, the sea, a pond, a well). Which?
3. (a) What was the *Countess*? (b) What was her captain's name?
4. The captain was like his name. What kind of man do you think he was?
5. What colours are mentioned: (a) for the sea (b) for the foam?
6. How far away was the other swimmer?
7. Why did Peter (a) open his mouth (b) close it again?
8. How did he keep his head out of the water?
9. What was the "tiny pinpoint of an object moving in the water"?
10. Explain: boiling, sizzle, propeller, surface, grip, whirlpool, sucked down again, green depths, choking, vanished, glassy sea, in the distance, pinpoint, faint.

B 1. Write down all the phrases which tell us that Peter was not a human being.

2. (a) Why was the water *roiling and boiling*? (b) Which *noun* in the extract means the same? (c) Was the water hot, boiling hot, cold or warm?
3. What did Peter do: desert Jennie, hold her up, shout for help, swim towards her?
4. Why did Peter's chest hurt?
5. How do you think Peter came to be in the water?
6. Why do you think Jennie was "perhaps fifty or sixty yards away"?
7. What made Peter believe that Jennie had seen him?
8. What was an even greater danger than drowning when Peter fell in?
9. (a) Why did Peter shout "Hold out."? (b) How would YOU *punctuate* it?
10. What is the meaning of: undertows, caught in the grip of, irresistible whirlpool, in the wake, no longer subject to, forces stirred up by her machinery, concentrate on reaching, in her direction, not minded to think about, losing precious time, two vagrant cats, a watery grave?

The Jervis Bay

To Messrs. Jones and Jubb she came, on the beating banks of Clyde,
And there in the dockyard's whelming din the civil liner died.
Down came the managers and draughtsmen, and the Admiralty Overseer,
With coats and plans and bowler hats and a brisk to-business air,
With "Yes, quite so . . ." and "What about . . ." and "Here's what I suggest,"
"The guns go here—the drawing's clear—we'll soon decide the rest."
Down came the dockyard mateys like locusts on the land,
The welders, fitters, joiners, a shambling happy band,
The plumbers and the shipwrights, the electricians came,
The riveters, the painters, the host no man can name.
They came in caps and oily coats with bags of tools and gear,
With drills and lamps and files and clamps and newspapers and beer,
They shuffled up the gangplanks, they lolled along the rails,
They stewed their tea on the galley stoves, they sat on upturned pails,
They joked and ate and smoked and met, and jostled each his neighbour,
Almost as though they did not know the dignity of labour.
They diced and dozed and took their ease, and viewed the job before them,
And found their way to nooks obscure before the charge hand saw them.
And yet, by some organic change, she sprouted here a gun
And there a bridge or rangefinder, till Presto! it was done.
A dockyard matey working was a sight you rarely saw;
Yet when they left the *Jervis Bay* she was a ship of war.

From *The Jervis Bay* by Michael Thwaites

Comprehension

A 1. What was the Jervis Bay?
2. Who were Messrs. Jones and Jubb?
3. What are dockyard "mateys"?
4. What work do these men do: (a) electrician (b) plumber (c) joiner?
5. (a) Who wore bowler hats?
(b) Does this kind of hat tell you anything special about the men?
6. Why did they visit the Jervis Bay?
7. What did the workmen (a) wear? (b) carry?
8. How could the Jervis Bay sprout guns?
9. What kind of bridge is mentioned?
10. Explain: din, liner, Admiralty, locusts, shambling, pails, gangplanks, dockyard, drills, files, clamps, the drawing's clear.

B 1. What happens to the Jervis Bay in this extract?
2. In which country does this happen?
3. (a) A charge hand is a kind of (bowler, matey, locust, foreman, nook). Which?
(b) Why is he so called?
4. Use your dictionary if necessary, to find out what work these men do:
(a) welders (b) fitters (c) shipwrights (d) riveters (e) draughtsmen.
5. Why should the workmen come "like locusts on the land"?
6. (a) Why is "shuffled" in line 13 a vivid word? (b) Use it in a sentence.
7. Explain: "Almost as though they did not know the dignity of labour."
8. Which two lines tell us that although the workmen wasted time they completed their task in the end?
9. Find as many verbs as possible which show the men wasting time. In some you will have to give whole phrases.
10. Explain: the beating banks of Clyde, whelming din, the civil liner died, coats and plans and bowler hats, a brisk to-business air, the host no man can name, caps and oily coats, they lolled along the rails, stewed their tea, the galley stoves, jostled each his neighbour, diced, viewed the job before them, found their way to nooks obscure, range-finder.
Find out what an "organic change" is.

13 *Language*

1. Say which preposition you would put into the gap in each sentence:
   (i) I am going —— my Aunt's house.
   (ii) The bird fell —— the roof.
   (iii) My sister's coat is different —— mine.
   (iv) I am thoroughly ashamed —— you.

2. ORIGINS OF WORDS Most words have very interesting origins (where they came from). Here are the origins of some words from the Comprehension extract from the poem "The Jervis Bay":
   Admiralty: from an old Arabic word *amir*, a prince or commander.
   plumber: from the Latin word *plumbum*, lead (lead piping, etc.).
   neighbour: from the Anglo-Saxon word *neahgebur*, a "near-person".

   Did you know that the word CANTER, a slow gallop, is an abbreviation of *Canterbury gallop*, the easy pace of the pilgrims who went on horseback to Canterbury in medieval times; or that a football JERSEY is named after the Channel Island of *Jersey*?

   Why do you think a raincoat is called a *mackintosh* and long rubber boots are called *wellingtons*?

   Try to find the origins of the following words. Most large dictionaries, like the Concise Oxford Dictionary, give origins, but in case you have no such dictionary available, a jumbled list of answers is given, so that you can try to work out each word's origin. First find the meaning of each word:
   bayonet, bus, calico, canary, cardigan, china, currants, damsons, guinea, tarmac, port-wine, sandwich, sardines, turkey.

   Origins: Latin *omnibus* (for all); Atlantic *Canary Isles*; *Guinea-gold*, Africa; *tar Macadam*; wrongly believed from *Turkey*; invented by an Earl of *Sandwich*; *Oporto*, Portugal; *Sardinia* in the Mediterranean Sea; *Bayonne*, France; *China*; an Earl of *Cardigan*; *Calicut-cloth*, India; *Damascus-plum*, Syria; *Corinth-raisins*, Greece.

3. *Find the Stranger*. Jones Smith Clyde Green White

4. Note the abbreviation "Messrs." in the first line of the extract. This is from a French word and means "Misters".
   What is the meaning of these abbreviations connected with ships: A.1, H.M.S., S.S., R.N., A.B.?

5. (a) Find twelve workmen in the Comprehension extract from *The Jervis Bay*.
   (b) What kind of work do these people do: blacksmith, cabinet-maker, caretaker, carpenter, chauffeur, chemist, cobbler, commercial traveller, draper, apprentice, florist, magistrate, auctioneer?
6. Use in interesting sentences of your own:
   the adjectives formed from: labour, dignity;
   the nouns formed from: civil, suggest, decide;
   the verbs formed from: managers, the drawing.
7. *Spelling* IE or EI? Some have other missing letters as well.
   n . . ther one nor the other; during the r . . . n of Queen Anne; rec . . ve; fr . . ndly natives; shouting and shr . . king; my next-door n . . . . bour; for . . . n travel (abroad); a p . . ce of cake; uncle and n . . ce; c . .ling; an anc . . nt castle; a f. . rce dog; s . . . e (grab) the stick; very vain: conc. . ted; s. . . . of a town (surrounded, being starved into surrender).
8. Think of nouns of sound to fit these: thunder (i. near ii. distant), a small bell, a cathedral bell, a horse, hoofs, rusty hinges, brakes, a gentle breeze, a gale, fire, rain, crockery, a torrent.
9. Think of words which sound exactly the same but which are spelt differently: draught, beer, pails, not, jam, kernel, key, knave, lane, leak.
   Give the meaning of your words.
10. (a) Which words in the poem rhyme with Clyde, rest, neighbour, saw?
    (b) Which of these words rhymes with GREAT: fate, treat, sleigh, greet?
11. Choose the correct words from those in the brackets:
    (a) Lazy people are not (idle, industrious, inactive, slothful).
    (b) The (guilty, blameless, innocent, executed) man was sent to prison.
    (c) "Your help was (valuable, valueless, invaluable)," said the grateful climber after he had been rescued.
    (d) Crops grew well on the (barren, hostile, fertile, treeless) plain.
    (e) We could not raise the (wet, damp, watery, waterlogged, ruined) boat.
12. How do we speak when we mumble, mutter, yell, whisper, bawl, exclaim, insist, falter, gabble, stammer, plead, converse, chat, complain, sneer?
13. Use these adverbs in short sentences: noisily, wearily, steeply, proudly, everywhere, soon.
14. Put into alphabetical order: she, ship, sight, saw, sprout, smoke, sat, soon.
15. Give the singular of Messrs., draughtsmen, managers, thieves, tomatoes.

16. What are the missing words: good, better, best: bad, ——, ——?
17. Use in sentences: banks of Clyde in the dockyard bowler hats like locusts in caps and oily coats upturned pails.

Find Out

1. Find out what these words mean, then use one from each group in sentences:
   civil, civilian, civility, civilisation over, overseer, oversight
   plum, plumb, plume, plump, plumbing galley, gallery, galleon, gallantry
   jostling, jousting bridge, bride, bridegroom, bridal, bridle, bribe, briar
   finder, founder, foundry, foundation, foundling obscure, obsolete, obstruct.
2. Find the meaning of: take after someone, take someone in, take someone off, take on, take to; ship's company, ship of the desert, ship of the line, shipmate, shipwreck, all shipshape and Bristol fashion, ship water, when my ship comes in, Don't spoil the ship for a ha'porth of tar.
3. *Workers: -er* Make a list of workers ending in ER, starting with those in the poem-extract, "The Jervis Bay". Describe each kind of work.
4. *Shipbuilding* Find out about shipbuilding and British shipyards.
   What are these: caulking, keel, fitting-out basin, maiden voyage, rivets, slipway, foundries, acetylene cutters, riggers, strakes?

List of Poems

The Jervis Bay by Michael Thwaites.
Song of the Wooden-legged Fiddler; Old Grey Squirrel by Alfred Noyes.
The Stormy Petrel by Barry Cornwall.
The Ship by Richard Church.
Sea Memories; The Secret of the Sea by H. W. Longfellow.
A Passer-by by Robert Bridges.
The Mayblossom by John Masefield.
A Ship Sails up to Bideford by Herbert Asquith.
Sailor's Delight by C. Fox Smith.
Chorus of the Homecoming Ships by Alfred Austin.

Comprehension comes at the end of this exercise.

14 *Language*

1. Give each flower the origin of its name and say why you think each one had such an origin, like this: *Azaleas* like a dry soil and have dry stems, so the ancient Greeks called this flower *azalea* from their word *azaleos* meaning *dry*.

   Flowers: rhododendron, anemone, azalea, crocus, dandelion, hyacinth.

   Origins: French *dent de lion* (lion's tooth), Greek *azaleos* (dry), Greek *anemone* (daughter of the wind), Greek *huakinthos* (flower and gem), Greek *rhodon dendron* (rose-tree), Greek *krokos* (saffron or yellow).

2. COMPARATIVE AND SUPERLATIVE DEGREE "Here was a chaos . . . even *worse* than in South Street . . . His *nearest* way lay through the churchyard . . ."

   bad, worse, worst   near, nearer, nearest

   Sometimes we compare two things and say that one is better, worse, nearer, etc. OR we compare more than two and say that one is the best, worst, nearest, etc.

   Remember: (1) Comparing TWO: nearer: COMPARATIVE degree.
   (2) Comparing MORE: nearest: SUPERLATIVE degree.

   This is the better of the two books.
   This is the best book of all.

   Do NOT say: more brighter, most brightest, better than me.
   Say: brighter, brightest, better than I (am).

   What are the Comparatives and Superlatives of fast, bad, good, quiet, pretty, slim?

   What is wrong with these Comparatives and Superlatives:

empty	emptier	emptiest
full	fuller	fullest
dead	deader	deadest?

3. *Find the Stranger* (a) windows roofs door inn wall
   (b) troops townspeople crowd folk sergeant

4. (a) Change to Direct Speech:
   Simon asked the sergeant why the soldiers were searching among the ruins.

   (b) Change to Indirect Speech:
   "I have orders to deliver this dispatch to General Fairfax," Simon told the sentry.

5. Which animals give us veal, venison, mutton, pork, ham, bacon, beef?

6. (a) Write correctly:

    (i) The bird fell (off, of, out) the branch.

    (ii) Divide this cake (among, between) six children.

    (iii) The scared kitten ran (out, out of, off, of) the room.

   (b) Use these four prepositions in one or more sentences: with, among, of, under.

7. "Simon walked on, turning up into the square."

   (a) What are the abbreviations in addresses, etc., for: Square, Road, Street, Crescent, Avenue, Drive, Gardens, Place, Terrace?

   (b) Draw an envelope and write your parents' name and address on it, taking care to start about half-way down.

8. *Spelling* (a) opposite of depth: h..... (b) fierce: fer...... (c) way in: ent..... (d) sad: mel....... (e) strange: cu..... (f) a current of ele........ (g) not clear: obs.... (h) what one decides: dec..... (i) noun from *destroy:* d.s.....ion (j) came near: app.......

9. Choose the correct words:

    (i) (Practice, Practise) hard if you wish to succeed.

    (ii) This shop is called an "Off (Licence, License)".

    (iii) Is that the best (advice, advise) you can offer?

    (iv) "I (prophecy, prophesy) seven years of famine," said Joseph.

10. If the pair of words are opposites, write O; if they are of similar meaning, write S: (i) arrival, departure (ii) order, chaos (iii) friend, foe (iv) distrust, mistrust (v) deliver, receive (vi) hideous, horrible (vii) desolate, ruined (viii) transparent, opaque.

11. Think of words which sound exactly the same but which are spelt differently: seen, whose, bare, here, guilt, hail, hair, hall, heel, heard.
    Give the meaning of your words.

12. Sort out these jumbled pairs so that there are no longer two strangers together, like this: horse, church; spire, stable: *horse, stable; spire, church*

Square, note	church, south	turf, troop	north, grass
trees, cloudy	soldiers, spire	fire, branches	sky, fly
rooks, burns	messenger, Avenue		

13. (a) Which of these are feminine: drake, ewe, goose, lioness, boar, buck, stallion, negress, vixen, tiger?

    (b) Say what the masculine is of the ones which you have chosen.

14. Use these words and phrases in short sentences, putting several into one sentence, if you wish: Margaret and I, ourselves, their, who, to John and me.
15. What is a conjunction? Use two in sentences.
16. Use in sentences: into the square blown-out windows the General's Troop in some farm buildings two old shops roofless.

Find Out

1. Find out what these words mean, then use one from each group in sentences:
   deliver, delirious, delicious, deliberate, delicate, delusion
   ancient, antique, antiques, anticipate, antarctic, antelope, anthracite
   stripped, striped, stropped urge, surge, verge, dirge, merge, purge, urgent.
2. Find the meaning of: square accounts with someone, all square, a square deal, a square meal; in someone's black books, pitch-black, jet-black, a brow as black as thunder, blackmail, the Black Maria, the Black Country (why?), the Black Death (why?), things look black, black diamonds, black and blue, black looks, the black sheep, put in black and white.
3. *Workers: -ent or -ant* Make two lists of workmen ending in ENT, like superintendent, and ANT, like sergeant. Say what kind of work they do.
4. *Counties* Find out about the counties of ONE of these: England, Scotland, Wales or Ireland: their chief towns, rivers, industries, etc.

   What are the English counties which do not have *shire* at the end of their names?

Book List

Simon; The Armourer's House; Brother Dusty-Feet; The Queen Elizabeth Story by Rosemary Sutcliff.
Plain Jane; Place Mill by Barbara Softly.
Children of the New Forest by Captain Marryat.
Cue for Treason; Grey Adventurer; Trumpets in the West by Geoffrey Trease.
Captain of Foot; Captain of Dragoons by Ronald Welch.
Gamble for a Throne by Henry Garnett.
Hounds of the King; The Children's Crusade by Henry Treece.
Ferry the Fearless by Carola Oman.
Down the Long Stairs by Winifred Cawley.

14 *An Unexpected Sight*

Simon walked on, turning up into the square. Here was a chaos of blown-out windows and stripped roofs, even worse than in South Street. Here also was a great coming and going of troops, wagons rolling in and horses being urged through the crowd. But scarcely any of the townspeople were to be seen, for though the good folk of Torrington had always been for Parliament, they had seen enough of armies in the past four years to distrust all of them, and they were keeping within doors.

Simon delivered up his dispatch to Fairfax in an upper room of the inn which he had taken over for his headquarters, and was ordered to join himself for the present to the General's Troop, which was quartered with the Third in some farm buildings on the north of the town. His nearest way lay through the churchyard, which had always been a thoroughfare from one part of the town to the other, and when he reached the head of the Square, and turned in between two old shops that seemed oddly crumbled and askew, he felt for an instant as though he had walked into some hideous dream.

His eyes had been ready for the quiet of leaning headstones, ancient lime trees among whose bare topmost branches the rooks would be at their building, the grey well-remembered church with its friendly little leaded spire . . . But the rooks had flown from trees that were no more than blasted stumps stretching here and there a broken limb to the clouding sky, or lying uprooted across the hummocked turf. The old houses that had ringed the place were broken back, empty-windowed, roofless, with here and there a great breach in a tottering wall. And the church? The church was a fire-blackened and desolate shell, piled with rubble, among which soldiers were searching, under the orders of a sergeant.

From *Simon* by Rosemary Sutcliff

Comprehension

This story, like the one in Exercise 8, is set in England during the Civil War, over 300 years ago.

A 1. Who had just come from South Street?
2. Describe the church, as Simon saw it.
3. Why did the people of Torrington stay at home?
4. (a) Who carried a message? (b) To whom? (c) Where?
5. (a) Where was the General's Troop? (b) What was the General's name?
6. Which was the shortest way to the farm?
7. (a) Was Simon dreaming? (b) How do you know?
8. Where were soldiers searching?
9. Who was in charge of these soldiers?
10. Explain: the square, chaos, blown-out windows, stripped roofs, coming and going, troops, wagons, scarcely any, distrust, delivered, leaning headstones, ancient, blasted stumps, uprooted, roofless, rubble, sergeant.

B 1. Why do you think there was "chaos" everywhere?
2. On whose side were the people of Torrington in this war?
3. Was this at the beginning of a war? Give a reason for your answer.
4. To whom do "he" and "his" refer in this sentence: "Simon delivered up *his* dispatch to Fairfax in an upper room of the inn which *he* had taken over for *his* headquarters . . ."?
5. (a) Which part of Torrington was very busy? (b) Why?
6. What would you guess to be the special duty of the Troop which was quartered (staying for a while) in the farm buildings?
7. Where were (a) the lime-trees? (b) two old shops? (c) tottering walls?
8. What part of the year was it and how do you know?
9. Describe the church as it had been before the war.
10. Explain: urged through the crowd, the good folk, had always been for Parliament, dispatch, headquarters, thoroughfare, oddly crumbled and askew, some hideous dream, His eyes had been ready for . . . ., rooks . . . at their building, friendly little leaded spire, broken limb, hummocked turf, ringed the place, a great breach, desolate shell.

15 *Poachers in Flight*

He did not care what might happen. The steadiness of the sounds of pursuit behind him did not matter.

Gradually the heavy fragrance of spruce-bark diminished and faded away. The park, after the intense blackness of the woods, seemed dangerously light under the clear starlight. It began to seem of vast extent also. They seemed already to have been running for many miles and during many hours.

He was running now on his second wind and the sweat was beginning to come out on his face. The sounds behind them had already diminished and long before the wall of the park appeared before them in the darkness they had ceased altogether. Without them the night silence seemed illimitable. There was something also ominous about it too.

Until they reached the wall it was broken only by the sound of their own feet in the grass and by the noise of Bishop spitting and snorting at intervals as he renewed his breath. At the wall they awoke again the rustle of dead leaves under the belt of trees, the flutter and scuffle of odd rabbits and birds. Once they were on the other side of the wall they, too, were silent.

Out on the road Bishop ran on implacably, turning to the right without pausing. He had reverted now to the old pace. The stars of the Plough lay half-over on the left hand of the men, very bright through the half-bare tree branches spreading and meeting over the little road. Under the trees it was very warm, the air damp and sultry as if with summer thunder. The men ran without speaking, one behind another, Bishop leading, always on the roadside grass.

They ran on thus for a great distance, leaving the first road for a second and that in turn for another and then another, forking and zigzagging through the belts of spruce and pine without pausing or speaking or changing their pace, the North Star always in front of them.

From *The Poacher* by H. E. Bates

Comprehension

A 1. How many men were there?
2. What are they doing, in this extract?
3. Was it light, dark, very dark or pitch dark in the woods?
4. What scent or smell slowly faded?
5. Who ran in front?
6. What happened to the noise behind them?
7. How did they find a way out of the park?
8. What did they find outside the park?
9. What did the men say to each other?
10. Explain: pursuit, gradually, fragrance, starlight, ceased, the night silence, snorting, odd rabbits and birds, damp and sultry, for a great distance, zigzagging, belts of spruce and pine.

B 1. (a) Why were the men running? (b) Where had they run from?
2. (a) What had they been doing? (b) What tells us?
3. (a) How can you tell that they did not like the lightness of the park? (b) Why do you think they did not like it?
4. Why do you think Bishop ran on the roadside grass?
5. (a) They were running (North, South, East, West) on the road. Which? (b) How do you know?
6. What time of the year was it? (Be careful!)
7. Explain fully the meaning of this sentence: "Once they were on the other side of the wall they, too, were silent."
8. Complete this sentence about the extract: —— and his son were chased by a —— while out one —— in the woods, —— ing. (Guess, if necessary.)
9. Which phrase best tells us that the two men were very good runners?
10. Explain: sounds of pursuit, heavy fragrance of spruce-bark, of vast extent, running now on his second wind, The sounds . . . had already diminished, renewed his breath, reverted now to the old pace, the Plough, ran on implacably (the adjective "implacable" means "determined, unrelenting"), the night silence seemed illimitable (Think of "legal" and "*il*legal" as a clue to help you.), something also ominous about it.

15 *Language*

1. Write correctly:

    (i) I was offered two books, so I accepted the (newer, newest) one of the two.

    (ii) I have a brother but I am the (oldest, older, eldest, elder).

    (iii) John writes better than (me, I).

    (iv) I think this flower is (lovelier, loveliest) than that one.

2. CONJUNCTIONS

What is a conjunction? Think of a railway junction: a joining up.

(a) "He was running now on his second wind *and* the sweat was beginning to come out on his face."

Note how the conjunction *and* joins together two sentences to make one.

(b) Use these conjunctions to join or complete the sentences given: until, before, after, and, but, if, unless, neither . . . nor, although, because.

Use each conjunction once only. You may have to alter other words.

(i) The man walked to the football match. His son walked with him.

(ii) I have tried hard. I cannot do it. (Two ways: conjunction in front; conjunction in the middle).

(iii) The steward knocked. The steward opened the door.

(iv) —— the servant had opened the door, she switched on the light.

(v) The woman was not there. Her daughter was not there.

(vi) I will give you this reward. I like your work.

(vii) I was determined to wait —— you arrived.

(viii) I shall have to let go, —— you help me quickly.

(ix) Tell me early —— you wish to go with me.

Remember: (1) Do NOT put a comma before *and*.

(2) When the second part is unexpected, use *but*:

We expected to win but were disappointed.

(3) I will try *and* come with you WRONG try *to* come: RIGHT.

(4) Do NOT begin sentences with *and* or *but*.

3. *Find the Stranger* warm thunder sultry damp wet

4. Give the opposite of gradually, heavy, intense, clear, vast, appeared, ceased, darkness, silence, at intervals, bright, damp, summer, leading.

5. What are these places: cathedral, aviary, surgery, stadium, ice-rink, cinema, theatre, plantation, reservoir, vineyard?

6. (a) Put these in order, the slowest first:

run crawl march saunter race

(b) What is the difference in meaning between: stroll, stride, creep, hobble, scurry and shuffle?

7. Write correctly:

(i) bishop and his son luke ran out of the woods across the park and out onto the road to escape from the gamekeeper

(ii) john smith and his son jack ran out of hargreaves wood across home park and out onto the nottingham road to escape from old willis the gamekeeper

(iii) stop stop shouted tom willis the gamekeeper ill have the law on you you thieving poachers

8. Think of interesting adjectives to go in the gaps. The sentences are not connected with what happens in the Comprehension extract.

(i) In the —— darkness the woods were —— and ——.

(ii) The —— park was surrounded by ——, —— walls.

(iii) The —— runners longed to see their —— cottage again.

9. Think of words which sound exactly the same but which are spelt differently: side, there, heir, herd, hew, higher, him, board, horse, hole.

Give the meaning of your words.

10. *Spelling* (a) cannot happen: imp....... (b) very great joy: ecs.... (c) almost, nearly: app..x..... (d) opposite of bravery: cow...... (e) a collection of poems: ant...... (f) a joiner, woodworker: car...... (g) teaching: ins.....ion (h) teacher: ins....... (i) joy given by something: enj...... (j) a happening: occ.......

11. Complete this table:

dawn morning midday afternoon —— night midnight
spring summer —— winter
January —— March April May
Monday —— —— Thursday Friday ——
freezing cold warm hot ——
million thousand —— ten
unconcerned alert alarmed frightened ——

12. What kind of work is done by: journalists, lawyers, athletes, carpenters, cashiers, typists, coastguards, glaziers, opticians, florists?

13. Complete these: a —— of ships, a —— of cards, a —— of flowers (2 different answers), a packet of ——, a grove of ——, a volley of ——, a clutch of ——, a bale of ——, a flight of ——.
14. What do these abbreviations stand for: I'd, doesn't, we've, who's, can't, shan't?
15. Write sentences, using (i) *belts* as a noun (ii) *spruce* as an adjective (iii) *light* as a verb (iv) *clear* as a verb.
16. Use in sentences: sounds of pursuit heavy fragrance dangerously light the night silence the rustle of the Plough.

Find Out

1. Find what these words mean, then use one from each group in sentences: reverted, inverted, diverted, converted ceased, creased, increased, decreased pursue, ensue, ensure, insure right, rite, write, wright, Wright hours, ours, hour's breath, breathe, breathless, breadth, bread, breach.
2. Find the meaning of: the breath of life, in the same breath, wasting one's breath, under one's breath, one's last breath, breathe freely again, a breathing-space, a breather, a breath of fresh air, hold one's breath in suspense, out of breath, Keep your breath to cool your porridge.
3. *Movement* 3 Make a list of verbs of "stationary movement" (movement while remaining in one place), like shiver, beckon and kneel. Explain each one.
4. *Woods* Find out about woods: (a) names of trees (b) names of "collections of trees". What is the difference between a clump, a copse, an avenue, etc.?

Book List

Trees in Britain by S. R. Badmin.
A Pocket-book of British Trees by E. H. B. Boulton.
British Trees by Hall and Jay.
How to Recognise Trees of the Countryside by Eric Pochin.
The Observer's Book of Trees and Shrubs of the British Isles by W. J. Stokoe.
Trees and Bushes in Wood and Hedgerow by H. Vedel and J. Lange.
Wayside and Woodland Trees by Edward Step.
The Shell Guide to Trees by Geoffrey Grigson.
Wild Flowers in Colour by John Hutchinson.
Flowers of the Wood by F. M. Day.

Comprehension comes at the end of this exercise.

16 *Language*

1. Use conjunctions to complete or to join up these sentences:
   (i) Ready thought the island was a long way off —— it was low.
   (ii) —— Mr. Seagrave —— Ready knew where they were.
   (iii) —— Mr. Seagrave was at the helm, Ready was examining the sea ahead.
   (iv) The helmsman peered ahead. He could not see any sign of land.
2. APOSTROPHE "... the ship's head ..."
   The *apostrophe* (') shows who owns something: the ship's head: the head of the ship; the girl's new frock: the new frock belonging to the girl.
   Remember: (1) Singular noun: add 's: boy: boy's books
   (2) Plural noun ending in s: add ': boys: boys' books
   (3) Plural noun not ending in s: add 's: men: men's books
   As a check, ask "Who owns it?" and place the apostrophe after the owner:
   The mans car: Who owns it? The *man*: the man's car.
   The mens game: Who owns it (or are connected with it)? The men: the men's game.
   Insert the apostrophe in these phrases: the dogs dinner, the two dogs dinner, the three mens cases, the childs bed, the childrens games, the womans passport, the womens magazines, a wolfs howling, spies disguises, a flys wings, flies wings, a Mens Club.
3. *Find the Stranger* land rock beech ground reefs shore
4. Correct Ready's mistake: "... to the windward of these sort of isles."
5. What is the difference in meaning between: occasionally, frequently, seldom, repeatedly? Use one in a sentence.
6. Give words of similar meaning: imagined, faster, water, cleft, taken ground, agitating, intelligent, mad.
7. Change Mr. Seagrave's answer in the Comprehension extract into Indirect Speech.
8. Change to (a) nouns: distant, deep, imagined, appeared, joined
   (b) adjectives: occasionally, think, spot, colour, usually
   (c) adverbs: clear, close, safety, steep
   (d) verbs: deep, cleft, satisfaction.
9. What do these words mean: course, coarse; raised, razed; current, currant;

stationary, stationery; council, counsel; crews, cruise; missed, mist; gamble, gambol; hoard, horde; higher, hire; muscle, mussel?

Remember: current (*e* for *e*lectricity) and station*e*ry (*e* for *e*nvelopes).

10. Complete this table by giving the person (any ending) and his action:

Example:	helm	helmsman	steers the ship
	piano	——	——
	suit of clothes	——	——
	island	——	——
	dock	——	——
	horseshoes	——	——
	residence	——	——

11. Complete these collections or groups: people in church or chapel: ——; a covey of ——; a —— of thieves; an —— of poems; a —— of piglets; a —— of birds; a squadron of ——; a volley of ——.
12. Write correctly: captain frederick marryat wrote several novels after service in the royal navy born in westminster in 1792 he entered the royal navy in 1806 rose to high rank retired in 1830 then wrote a series of novels peter simple mr midshipman easy masterman ready and the children of the new forest are still popular he died in 1848
13. Insert suitable adverbs:
    (i) The runners staggered —— along the long, dusty road.
    (ii) The mischievous boys tiptoed —— down the dark corridor.
    (ii) She picked up the kitten very ——, stroked it ——, then placed it very —— in its basket.
14. Give the singular of: brethren, children, cargoes, loaves, women, tomatoes, keys, men-o'-war, salmon, handfuls.
15. *Spelling* (a) lessen, become less: dim..... (b) dodging about: zig...... (c) scampering: scu...... (d) shiver: shu.... (e) very large in area: ext...... (f) not safely: dan........ (g) pulled up by the roots: up...... (h) full stops, commas, etc.: pun........ (i) spare time: l...ure (j) generous: lib....
16. Put into alphabetical order: distant, degrees, dock, deep, beach, drop, beech
17. What is the meaning of masculine and feminine? Give an example of each.
18. Use in sentences: he had imagined a low coral island groves of an agitating moment the beach four miles.

Find Out

1. Find what these words mean, then use one from each group in sentences:
   helmsman, helm, helmet, pelmet, pellet, pell-mell, pelican   to steer, a steer
   degrees, decrees   groves, graves, grooves   underground, undergrowth
   a fathom, to fathom   plumb-line, plumbing, plumber, plumb, plumage, plunge.
2. Find the meaning of: weather-beaten, make heavy weather, under the weather, weather a storm, a weathercock, keep one's weather-eye open, April weather, fair or foul weather, seasonable weather, weather-bureau, weather-forecast, weather-glass, weather-ship, weather-vane.
3. *Double Letters* Make a list of pairs of words like grove, gr*oo*ve; hoping, ho*pp*ing; holy, ho*ll*y, etc. Give their meaning.
4. *Ships* Find out about ships of the Royal Navy and the Merchant Navy.
   What are these: cruisers, lascars, P. & O., Cunard White Star, Trinity House, the QE2, the Canberra, the Mercantile Marine, destroyers, frigates, submarines, petty officers, commodores, radar?

Book List

Masterman Ready; Peter Simple; Mr. Midshipman Easy by Captain Marryat.
Blackadder by John Keir Cross.
The Lame Duck; Danger Rock; Sea Change; The Lost Ship by Richard Armstrong.
Blow the Man Down by Charles Vipont.
Bird of Dawning by John Masefield.
Sixteen Sail in Aboukir Bay by Stephanie Plowman.
The Observer's Book of Ships by F. E. Dodman.
The Story of Ships by S. E. Ellacott.
The Ship's Crew by A. B. Cornwell.
Ship's Captain by Eric Leyland.
The Hawk by Ronald Welch.

16 *Running Ashore*

Ready went to the helm and steered a course for the land, which was not so far distant as he had imagined, for the island was very low. By degrees the wind freshened up, and they went faster through the water; and now the trees, which had appeared as if in the air, joined on to the land, and they could make out that it was a low coral island covered with groves of cocoa-nuts. Occasionally Ready gave the helm up to Mr. Seagrave, and went forward to examine.

When they were within three or four miles of it, Ready came back from the forecastle and said: "I think I see my way pretty clear, sir. You see we are to the windward of the island, and there is always deep water to the windward of these sort of isles, and reefs and shoals to leeward. We must, therefore, find some little cleft in the coral rock to dock her in, as it were, or she may fall back into deep water after she has taken ground; for sometimes these islands run up like a wall, with forty or fifty fathom of water close to the weathersides of them; but I see a spot where I think she may be put on shore with safety. You see those three cocoa-nut trees close together on the beach? Now, sir, I cannot well see them as I steer, so do you go forward, and if I am to steer more to the right, put out your right hand, and if to the left, the same with your left; and when the ship's head is as it ought to be, then drop the hand which you have raised."

"I understand, Ready," replied Mr. Seagrave, who then went forward and directed the steering of the vessel as they neared the island. When they were within half a mile of it the colour of the water changed, very much to the satisfaction of Ready, who knew that the weatherside of the island would not be so steep as was usually the case; still it was an agitating moment as they ran on to the beach.

From *Masterman Ready* by Captain Marryat

Comprehension

A 1. What does a ship's helmsman do?
2. They were heading towards (a mountain, a lake, an island, a port). Which?
3. How far were they from land when Ready came back from the forecastle?
4. (a) Were they to the leeward or windward of the island?
(b) The two words are opposites. What do you think *leeward* means?
5. (a) What did they have to find? (b) Why?
6. What did Ready use as a guide?
7. What was the signal to tell him that he was steering correctly?
8. What became different, half a mile from shore?
9. (a) Give another way of spelling "cocoa-nut". (b) What has it to do with cocoa?
10. What is the meaning of: imagined, appeared, examine, helm, occasionally, dock her, cleft?

B 1. (a) What is a forecastle? (b) How is it pronounced?
(c) What does *fore* mean in forecastle, forehead, forecast, etc.?
2. (a) What is coral? (b) What is a fathom?
3. What deceived Ready into thinking that the island was further away?
4. Why do you think the colour of the water changed?
5. What is another word in the extract for "weatherside"?
6. How can islands "run up like a wall"?
7. (a) Were the people on the ship afraid? (b) When? (c) Why?
8. What happened to the ship, eventually?
9. Who do you think (a) Ready was? (b) Mr. Seagrave was?
10. Explain: steered a course, By degrees the wind freshened up, had appeared as if in the air, groves of cocoa-nuts, gave the helm up, went forward to examine, windward, leeward, reefs and shoals, after she has taken ground, directed the steering, to the satisfaction of Ready, an agitating moment.

17 A Ruined City

Beyond the square and the main street the city lay in complete ruin, in some places actually buried under mounds of earth on which not a blade of grass or other vegetation grew. Here and there were gaping chasms, and when the explorers dropped rocks into these not a sound came up to indicate bottom. There was little doubt now what had devastated the place. The Portuguese knew what earthquakes were and what destruction they could do. Here whole buildings had been swallowed, leaving perhaps only a few carved blocks to show where they had stood. It was not difficult to imagine something of the awful cataclysm that had laid waste this glorious place, tumbled columns and blocks weighing perhaps fifty tons and more, and that had destroyed in a matter of minutes the painstaking labour of a thousand years!

The far side of the square terminated in a river about thirty yards wide, flowing straight and easily from the north-west and vanishing in distant forest. At one time a fine promenade had bordered on the river, but the masonry was now broken up and much had subsided into the water. On the other side of the river were fields that were once cultivated, still covered with abundant coarse grass and a carpet of flowers. Rice had propagated and thrived in the shallow swamps all about, and here the waters were alive with duck.

Raposo and his party forded the river and crossed the swamps towards an isolated building about a quarter of a mile away, and the ducks scarcely troubled to move from their path. The building was approached by a flight of steps in stone of many colours, for it stood on a rise and its frontage extended for 250 paces. The imposing entrance, behind a square monolith with deeply engraved characters, opened into a vast hall where carvings and decorations had resisted the depredations of time in an amazing manner. They found fifteen chambers opening off the great hall, and in each was a carved serpent's head with a thin stream of water still flowing from it into the open mouth of another stone serpent beneath. The place could have been the college of a priesthood.

From *Exploration Fawcett* by Lt.-Col. P. H. Fawcett

Comprehension

A 1. What was lying in ruins?
2. Why did the explorers drop rocks?
3. (a) What is an earthquake? (b) What is the meaning of "destruction"?
4. How heavy were some blocks of stone?
5. How long had it taken to build the city?
6. (a) How broad was the river? (b) Where did it disappear?
7. (a) What is a promenade? (b) Where was the fine promenade?
8. What was growing in the marshy ground?
9. What was built at the top of a flight of multi-coloured steps?
10. What is the meaning of: the square, the main street, complete ruin, mounds of earth, vegetation, explorers, vanishing, distant forest, forded, entrance?

B 1. (a) Who was Raposo? (b) What was his nationality?
2. Why were there gaping chasms?
3. (a) What had destroyed the city? (b) Slowly or quickly?
4. What tells us that this city had been destroyed long ago?
5. The river flowed (North, South, East, West, S.E., N.W.). Which?
6. Why do you think the wild ducks were not afraid of the explorers?
7. How far do you think 250 paces would be?
8. (a) How many serpent's heads were there? (b) Why had they been built?
9. What is sad about the information at the end of the first paragraph?
10. What is the meaning of: gaping chasms, to indicate bottom, devastated, Portuguese, laid waste, columns, painstaking labour, terminated, bordered on, masonry, abundant, a carpet of flowers, alive with duck, frontage, extended, isolated, imposing entrance, engraved characters, college of a priesthood?

Find out the meaning of the harder phrases, like "propagated and thrived", "resisted the depredations of time", "square monolith", "awful cataclysm".

17 *Language*

1. Put the apostrophe into these sentences:
   (i) One barrows handles were missing.
   (ii) The mayors brief-case was stolen.
   (iii) Many boys shoes were dirty.
   (iv) The childrens toys were hidden behind the womens magazines.

2. GENDER There are four genders:
   (i) *masculine*, like king, man, bull
   (ii) *feminine*, like queen, woman, cow
   (iii) *common* (can be masculine or feminine), like owner, friend, baby
   (iv) *neuter* (neither masculine nor feminine), like car, wood, house.

   Give the gender of drake, river, duckling, duck.

   Complete this table:

Masculine	*Feminine*	*Common*	*Anything Neuter connected with them*
stag	hind	——	antlers
prince	——	R——	——
father	——	——	——
——	——	fox	——
——	——	pig	——
——	——	swan	——
——	——	horse	——

3. *Find the Stranger* Portugal Spain French Germany Italy
4. Use these words in sentences: frieze, receipt, recipe, siege.
5. Put suitable adverbs into these sentences:
   (i) The crafty fox crept —— round the farmyard. (Manner)
   (ii) The tired children went to bed ——. (Time)
   (iii) The explorers looked —— but could not find the path. (Place)
6. Put in order, the smallest first:
   city, country, hamlet, county, continent, town, universe, world, village.
7. Form nouns from: buried, indicate, devastated, carved, difficult, weighing, destroyed, terminated (2), wide, easily, cultivated, alive.
8. Think of words with the same or similar meaning: devastated, vanish, masonry, subside, abundant, isolated, imposing, forded, resist, terminate.

9. "deeply engraved characters"

What is the difference between engraved characters, a character in a play and a person's character?

10. Think of words which sound exactly the same but which are spelt differently: knew, manner, waste, time, coarse, steps, weighed, weigh, idle, isle.

Give the meaning of your words.

11. Complete this table:

earthquake, earth	:	eruption, ——
city, village	:	——, villagers
exploration, explorer	:	empire, ——
Portuguese, ——	:	——, Holland
terminate, end	:	——, begin
masonry, ——	:	building, builder
ducks, quack	:	——, gobble
entrance, ——	:	in, out
vast, tiny	:	ocean, ——

12. Change to the Past tense with "have", etc.:
   (i) The city lay for centuries in complete ruin.
   (ii) Not a blade of grass grew there.
   (iii) There was little doubt in their minds.
   (iv) The stream freezes every winter.
   (v) David slew Goliath.

13. *Spelling* (a) abruptly: sud..... (b) the inside: int..... (c) the outside: ext..... (d) not real: art....... (e) level with the horizon: hor....... (f) the opposite of (e): ver..... (g) disaster: cat........ (h) hanging: sus...... (i) troubles: har...... (j) sweet-smelling: fra.....

14. Change to the Present tense: where they had stood; had laid waste; had destroyed; terminated; had thrived; forded the river; lay in complete ruin.

15. What is the difference between a biography and an autobiography?

Which are these: (i) *Exploration Fawcett* by Lt-Col. P. H. Fawcett, about his own adventures
(ii) *The Life of John Smith* by William Jones?

16. What is the difference between these: stream, tributary, spring, source, torrent, river, rivulet, canal, channel, the English Channel, straits, the Straits of Dover, rapids, a burn, streamlet, cataract, waterfall, reservoir?

17. Use in sentences: the main street in complete ruin gaping chasms distant forest shallow swamps a square monolith.

Find Out

1. Find what these words mean, then use six in sentences: across, cross; Crosses: Maltese, St. Andrew's, St. George's, St. Patrick's, George, Victoria, Southern; a crossbow, crossroads, crossbill, crosspatch, cross-country race, cross-examine, cross-legged, at cross purposes.
2. Find the meaning of: word of mouth, river-mouth, mouthful, live from hand to mouth; in deep water, in hot water, like water off a duck's back, spend money like water, throw cold water on a plan, as weak as water, watermark, watershed, waterproof, Much water has flowed under the bridge.
3. *Sounds* 2 Make a list of sounds which are NOT made by living things and say what makes each one, like this: tinkle: tiny bell clang: large bell
4. *South America* Find the names of the countries of South America and the answers to the following question:

   What are these: gauchos, llamas, Pampas, the Andes, the Amazon, Brasilia, campos, tapirs, jaguars, estancias?

Book List

Exploration Fawcett by Lt.-Col. P. H. Fawcett.
With Colonel Fawcett in the Amazon Basin by Harry Williams.
See Through the Jungle by Millicent Selsam.
Amazon Adventures of Two Children; Two Children and their Jungle Zoo by Rose Brown.
Chico of the Andes by Christine von Hagen.
Dark Amazon by Martin Gregg.
Canga by J. A. Vaughn.
Frozen Fire by Armstrong Sperry.
Exploring the Americas by L. F. Hobley.
Cassell's Boy's Book of Exploration, edited by Sir Edmund Hillary.
River Boy by Ralph Hermanns.

Comprehension comes at the end of this exercise.

18 *Language*

1. What is the gender of duchess, buck, stag, hind, princess, monarch, ruler (for measuring), cat, sheep, ram, ewe, doe, vixen, tigress, cage, abbot, abbey?
2. SINGULAR AND PLURAL NUMBER

   Remember: (i) Singular (single) Plural (plus or more)

   (ii) Ways of forming plurals:

   (1) add S: rat, rats rabbit, rabbits girl, girls

   (2) add ES to words ending in S (glass, glasses), SH (brush, brushes), CH (church, churches), X (box, boxes)

   (3) change the ending F or FE to V and add ES: wolf, wolves wife, wives (Some words do not follow this rule: cliff, cliffs; chief, chiefs; etc.)

   (4) add S to words ending in a vowel and Y: day, days chimney, chimneys no vowel before Y, change Y to I and add ES: baby, babies lady, ladies

   (5) change the vowels in the middle: tooth, teeth man, men

   (6) end in EN: child, children ox, oxen

   (7) no change at all: deer, deer sheep, sheep

   Be careful with (a) words ending in O: piano, pianos solo, solos echo, echoes potato, potatoes tomato, tomatoes;

   and (b) compound words: son-in-law, sons-in-law passer-by, passers-by.

   Give the plural of: fairy, thief, calf, box, ox, handkerchief, hoof, dwarf, potato, piano, hero, chimney, mouse, sheep, brother-in-law, man-servant, passer-by.
3. *Note* the words concerning LIGHT in the extract from "London Snow": brightness, glare, dazzling, whiteness.

   (a) What part of speech is each word?

   (b) Change three of them so that they are all adjectives and write them down in order of brightness, the weakest first.

   (c) Put these sources of light in order, the dimmest first: candle, electric light, searchlight, match.
4. Write these phrases correctly: (out, out of) the window angry (at, with, to, of) him change places (with, for, from) me divide (between, among) two.
5. *Find the Stranger* men snow town flakes softly night
6. Use in sentences: lying, laying.

7. (a) Which words in the extract rhyme with lying, town, sailing, knees?
   (b) Which of these words rhymes with NEIGH: eight, neighbour, play, nigh?
8. Give the opposite of asleep, loosely, drowsy, lazily, silently, hiding, depth, brightness, dazzling, busy.
9. In the poem there is a crowd of boys going to school.
   Complete these collections: a —— of puppies, a —— of cows in a field, a —— of lions, a —— of monkeys, an —— of people in a theatre, a —— of people in church or chapel, a swarm of ——, a flock of ——, a covey of ——, a convoy of ——.
10. Think of words which sound exactly the same but which are spelt differently: veil, its, road, eye, nor, freeze, fair, feet, faint, find.
    Give the meaning of your words.
11. In the poem the boys are going to school to *learn*. Their teachers will *teach*.
    Remember: Teachers *teach*. You *learn*. You are *taught*.
    Write correctly:
    (i) That will (learn, teach) you a lesson!
    (ii) Their new teacher (learnt, learned, taught) them to be polite.
    (iii) Please will you (learn, teach) me how to ride a bicycle?
    (iv) We try to (learn, teach) all that our teachers try to (learn, teach) us.
12. What part of speech is each word: practice, practise, licence, license, advice, advise, prophecy, prophesy?
13. What do we call these places: (a) places of worship (several), a building in which cars are kept, where historical relics are on show, the railway station at the end of a main-line, where people pay to eat (several)?
    (b) the homes of dogs, foxes, lions, owls and badgers?
14. *Spelling* (a) in short: br...ly (b) go on: con..... (c) out of the ordinary: ext.......... (d) decide: det...... (e) the opposite of success: fa..... (f) work: emp....... (g) wonderful: mar....... (h) put out a light: ext....... (i) trustworthy: rel..... (j) uproar: com.....
15. Change the verbs to the Past tense with "have", etc.: (i) Birds are flying high. (ii) I arise early. (iii) She buys the best goods. (iv) The concert began earlier today. (v) He will forget about it. (vi) He wrote the letter very carelessly.
16. Use *three* of these conjunctions in sentences: since, till, but, because, either ... or, although, while
17. What is a prefix? Give an example.

18. Use in sentences: large white flakes stealthily frosty heaven dazzling whiteness busy morning cries crystal.

Find Out

1. Find what these words mean, then use one from each group in sentences:
   angles, Angles, angels asleep, askance, aback, ablaze, abound, abridge
   perpetual, perpendicular, permanent, perimeter, persistent, persecute, persevere
   incessant, incident, incomplete, incompetent, inconvenient, incorrect, incredible.
2. Find the meaning of: footnote, footman, footpad, footplate, footlights, foot the bill, put one's foot down firmly, feet of clay, stand on one's own feet, put one's best foot forward, put one's foot in it, hot-foot, on foot, foot-and-mouth disease.
3. *Brightness* An actor's acting may be *brilliant* but NOT *luminous*; a fire may be *blazing* but NOT *glossy*.

   Find out how to use these words: bright, brilliant, luminous, phosphorescent, scintillating, gleaming, sparkling, dazzling, glowing, glaring, shining, radiant, beaming, blazing, glittering, glossy, twinkling, burnished, flashing, shimmering.
4. *London* Collect information about London: famous buildings, the Thames, docks, parks, railway stations, etc.

   What are these: P.L.A., L.T.E., the Underground, Mme. Tussaud's, London clay, London pride, Londoners, Cockneys, Metropolitan Police, Eros, Nelson's Column, Cleopatra's Needle, Euston, Beefeaters, Big Ben, the Monument?

List of Poems

London Snow by Robert Bridges.
Snow in Town by Rickman Mark.
Snow in the Suburbs by Thomas Hardy.
Snow; The Shining Streets of London by Alfred Noyes.
Stopping by Woods on a Snowy Evening by Robert Frost.
Winter in the Fens by John Clare.
Winter the Huntsman by Osbert Sitwell.
Winter's Beauty by W. H. Auden.
Winter by Tennyson.
Winter by Walter de la Mare.

18

London Snow

When men were all asleep the snow camc flying,
In large white flakes falling on the city brown,
Stealthily and perpetually settling and loosely lying,
Hushing the latest traffic of the drowsy town;
Deadening, muffling, stifling its murmurs failing;
Lazily and incessantly floating down and down:
Silently sifting and veiling road, roof and railing;
Hiding difference, making unevenness even,
Into angles and crevices softly drifting and sailing.
All night it fell, and when full inches seven
It lay in the depth of its uncompacted lightness,
The clouds blew off from a high and frosty heaven;
And all woke earlier for the unaccustomed brightness
Of the winter dawning, the strange unheavenly glare:
The eye marvelled—marvelled at the dazzling whiteness;
The ear hearkened to the stillness of the solemn air;
No sound of wheel rumbling nor of foot falling,
And the busy morning cries came thin and spare.
Then boys I heard, as they went to school, calling,
They gathered up the crystal manna to freeze
Their tongues with tasting, their hands with snowballing;
Or rioted in a drift, plunging up to the knees;
Or peering up from under the white-mossed wonder.

From *London Snow* by Robert Bridges

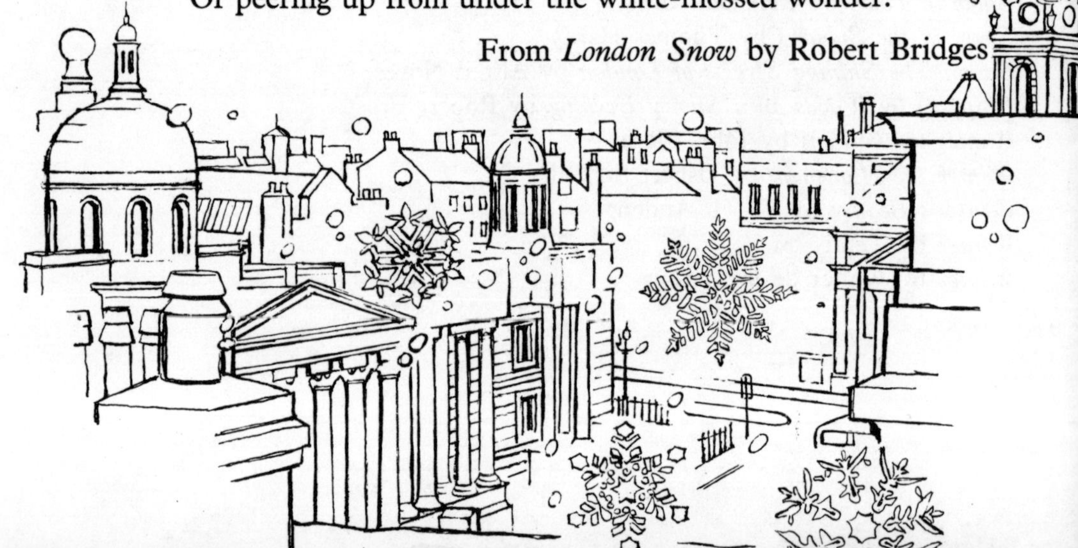

Comprehension

A 1. When did the snow fall?
2. How did white come down on brown?
3. Why was the city sleepy?
4. What did the snow quieten?
5. Which two adverbs tell us how the snowflakes came to rest?
6. Where did the snow drift?
7. (a) How long was it falling? (b) How deep was it?
8. Whom did the poet hear, the following morning?
9. What did the schoolboys do with the snow?
10. What do these words mean: hushing, drowsy, deadening, muffling, traffic, lazily, floating, depth, dawning, unaccustomed?

B 1. Where did this happen?
2. Why did people awake earlier than usual?
3. To what did the people listen?
4. What was a wonderful sight?
5. (a) What do you think were the busy morning cries?
(b) Why were they "thin and spare"?
6. Find seven actions of the boys.
7. Why is "rioted" more descriptive than "played" would be, in the next to the last line?
8. What do you think "its uncompacted lightness" means, if *compact* means "closely packed"?
9. The word *manna* means "food from Heaven". Why is "crystal manna" a very clever and fitting phrase?
10. What is the meaning of: the latest traffic, stealthily, perpetually, loosely lying, incessantly, veiling, making unevenness even, angles and crevices, unheavenly glare, white-mossed wonder, rioted in a drift?

19 *Hunted by an Enemy*

There was a sound like a twanged fiddle-string, and a bullet passed over my left shoulder. I felt the wind of it on my cheek.

The next second I was on my back wriggling below the sky-line. Once there I got to my feet and ran—up the ridge on my left to get a view from higher ground. The shot, so far as I could judge, had come from well below and a little to the east of where I had been standing. I found another knuckle of rock, and crept to the edge of it, so that I looked from between two boulders into the glen.

The place was still utterly quiet. My enemy was hidden there, probably not half a mile off, but there was nothing to reveal his presence. The light wind stirred the bog cotton, a merlin sailed across to Stob Coire Easain, a raven croaked in the crags, but these were the only sounds. There was not even a sign of deer.

My glass showed that half-way down an old ewe was feeding—one of those melancholy beasts which stray into a forest from adjacent sheep-ground, and lead a precarious life among the rocks, lean and matted and wild. They are far sharper-eyed and quicker of hearing than a stag, and an unmitigated curse to the stalker. The brute was feeding on a patch of turf near a big stretch of bracken, and suddenly I saw her raise her head and stare. It was the first time I had ever felt well disposed towards a sheep.

She was curious about something in a shallow gully which flanked the brackens, and so was I. I kept my glass glued on her, and saw her toss her disreputable head, stamp her foot, and then heard her whistle through her nose. This was a snag Medina could not have reckoned with. He was clearly in that gully, working his way upward in its cover, unwitting that the ewe was giving him away.

From *The Three Hostages* by John Buchan

Comprehension

A 1. What did the bullet sound like?
2. What did the man do immediately?
3. Why did the man run up to higher ground?
4. (a) Had his enemy fired up or down the mountain-side? (b) How do you know?
5. "My enemy was hidden there." What was the enemy's name?
6. (a) Explain "My glass". (b) How could it "show" something?
7. (a) What was a sad animal? (b) Can you think why?
8. Why did the animal stare, shake her head and stamp?
9. (a) Had Medina seen and heard the animal? (b) How do you know?
10. What is the meaning of: wriggling, sky-line, ridge, view, boulders, glen, utterly quiet, stirred, a merlin sailed across, a raven croaked in the crags, a sign of, stray, sharper-eyed, the brute, a patch of turf, bracken?

B 1. Why did the man wriggle below the sky-line?
2. Complete this: The man who felt the wind of the bullet on his cheek was about (how far?) (East, West, North, South) of the man with the rifle.
3. In which country do you think this happened? Explain your choice.
4. Why is a stag mentioned?
5. (a) What would you expect Stob Coire Easain to be? (b) Why?
6. (a) What is a stalker? (b) Who is one in the extract? (c) Who is being stalked?
7. Why should stray animals be a "curse to the stalker"?
8. Which sentence tells us that the man looking at the stray ewe usually found them to be nuisances?
9. What are three *hostages*?
10. Explain: a twanged fiddle-string, the wind of it, so far as I could judge, knuckle of rock, nothing to reveal his presence, melancholy beasts, adjacent sheep-ground, lead a precarious life, lean and matted, a shallow gully, flanked the brackens, a snag, unwitting, I kept my glass glued on her. *Use your dictionary* if you need help, especially with these difficult words: unmitigated curse, well disposed, disreputable.

19

Language

1. Give the plural of: church, hoof, roof, patch, brother-in-law, branch, turf, beech, dozen, deer, spoonful, passer-by, trout, oasis, species, ox, army, chief.

2. PREFIX A prefix is "pre-fixed" or placed at the front of a word to form a new word: head, *fore*head; script, *post*script; happy, *un*happy.
   Some prefixes form words of opposite meaning: im, in, un, dis, il, ir, non, etc.
   (a) Give a prefix to each word to form opposites: correct, possible, regular, sense, legal, probable, visible, seen, agree, appear.
   (b) Give words with the following prefixes and explain the work of the prefix, like this: subway (a way *under*: *sub* means *under*): bi, tri, sub, post, semi, trans, arch, re, ab, ad, circum.
   Remember: The letters *un*, *im*, *in*, *bi*, etc. at the beginning of a word are *not always* a prefix. The word *universe* is not formed by putting *un* in front of *iverse*; *bitter* is not *bi-tter;* etc.

3. *Find the Stranger* ewe stag lioness hind doe

4. Think of words which sound exactly the same but which are spelt differently: nose, deer, presence, alter, ascent, baron, berry, phrase, morning, birth. Give the meaning of your words.

5. Think of words (a) of similar meaning and (b) of opposite meaning:
   melancholy, precarious, quiet, suddenly, hidden, probably, quicker, lean.

6. Put into two groups, according to their meaning: ridge, glen, crags, gully, ravine, mountain, valley, peak, range, dale, hillock, mound, gorge, canyon, hummock.

7. (a) What do we call shopkeepers in these shops and what do they sell: millinery, confectionery, grocery, greengrocery, stationery shops?
   (b) Who sells fish, flowers, newspapers, meat?
   (c) Who catches rabbits, etc. without permission, carries suitcases for passengers at railway stations, makes and repairs locks, takes fares on buses, looks after patients in hospital?
   (d) What is the difference between a doctor and a surgeon?

8. ". . . wriggling below the skyline . . . ran . . . crept . . . a merlin sailed across . . . stray into a forest . . . working his way upward . . ."
   What kind of movement does each verb describe: (a) in the above list, (b) prowl, roam, strut, stroll, scurry, limp, crawl, march, hobble, stride, leap, climb, clamber, scramble?

9. Sort out these wrong pairs:
fiddle, mice   pupils, violin   bullet, bird   bells, babbling   merlin, rifle
horizon, sailor   mouse, tolling   Navy, teacher   brook, skyline.

10. Give another word which will not change the meaning of the sentence on the left:
Example: Can you do it? Are you *able* to do it?
(i) Is play probable today? Are we —— to play today?
(ii) The small boy decided to try. The small boy —— to try.
(iii) The soldiers were tired of captivity. The soldiers were tired of being ——ed.
(iv) The trees' foliage was turning red. The trees' —— were turning red.
(v) I must decide. I must make a ——.
(vi) Do not show ingratitude. Do not be ——.
(vii) He is a very cautious swimmer. He is a very —— swimmer.
(viii) The cyclist went slowly down the steep hill. The cyclist —— the steep hill slowly.

11. Change *all* singulars to plural:
(i) My enemy was hidden there.
(ii) There was not even a sign of deer.
(iii) An old ewe was feeding. This was the only sheep I could see.
(iv) I saw her toss her disreputable head, stamp her foot and whistle.

12. *Spelling* (a) help (noun): ass....... (b) buy; p.r..... (c) going on a journey: tra....... (d) opposite of wealth: po....y (e) hidden: con...... (f) the noun from *behave*: beh...... (g) thunder and li....... (h) not real: ima....ry (i) standing still: sta....... (j) worried: ala....

13. Put into Direct Speech:
(i) The man told the boy to go away.
(ii) The policeman told the crowd to move back.
(iii) The teacher asked the boy why he was late.
(iv) The singer said that her next song would bring the concert to an end.

14. Write correctly:
(i) in the three hostages by john buchan stob coire easain is mentioned
(ii) please (can, may) i (borrow, lend) your library book the three hostages i said

15. (a) Put in order, the gentlest first: breeze, gale, hurricane, squall.
(b) Think of other words like hurricane: cyclone, etc.

16. What is a suffix? Give an example.

17. Use in sentences: over my left shoulder up the ridge between two boulders in the crags a patch of turf curious.

Find Out

1. Find what these words mean, then use one from each group in sentences:
   a sound, astounded skyline, horizon, horizontal, vertical, diagonal
   cover, clover, glover, plover disposition, composition, preposition
   reveal, relieve, relive, revive sky, ski ewe, yew pitch, patch.
2. Find the meaning of: playing second fiddle, as fit as a fiddle, Fiddlesticks!, cheeky, turn the other cheek, knuckle under, a sharp rap on the knuckles, nose in the air, keep one's nose to the grindstone, pay through the nose, lead by the nose, as plain as the nose on your face, unable to see further than one's nose.
3. *Pre- Words* Find the meaning of words in which *pre* at the beginning makes the words mean *before* or *in front of* . . . like prefix, precede, prefect, etc.
4. *The British Isles* Make a list of the countries of the British Isles, their capitals and chief towns, then find out the answers to the following question:
   What and where are these: Holyrood, Tower Bridge, Land's End, John o' Groats, Anglesey, Londonderry, the Mersey Tunnel, Ben Nevis, Scotland Yard, Snowdon, Ulster, the Pennines? Explain: Eire.

Book List

The Three Hostages; The Thirty-Nine Steps by John Buchan.
Great Northern by Arthur Ransome.
House of the Pelican by Elizabeth Kyle.
House in Hiding by Elinor Lyon.
Young Man with a Sword; The Eaglet and the Angry Dove by Jane Oliver.
Peril in the Pennines by Winifred Finlay.
The World Upside-down; Follow the Footprints; Thumbstick by William Mayne.
Our Island Story; Scotland's Story by H. E. Marshall.
Village and Town by S. R. Badmin.
A Valley Grows Up by Edward Osmond.
Strange Valley by Mary Cockett.

Comprehension comes at the end of this exercise.

20 *Language*

1. Find out the meaning of these words, thereby finding out the meaning of their prefixes: readdress, rearrange, hemisphere, admire, admit, a duologue, a monologue, a bicycle, a tricycle, a submarine, a subway.
2. SUFFIX In Exercise 19 we talked about prefixes. The opposite is a *suffix*. The word *suffix* comes from *sub-fix* (fixed under, meaning *behind*):
   care, care*less*, care*ful* glory, glori*ous* lion, lion*ess*
   Suffixes: less (without) ful (full of) ous (full of) ess (female).
   (a) *Note* the spelling of these words with the suffix *able*:
   movable, serviceable, changeable.
   What do these words mean? What does the suffix *able* mean?
   (b) Which adjective ending in the suffix *ible* means "eatable"?
   (c) From the meaning of the whole word say what special meaning the suffix has in these words, the first one being done as an example for you:
   observat*ory* (a place where one observes or watches something, so the suffix *ory* means "a place where . . .")
   dormit*ory* (the beginning of this word means "sleeping"), six*teen*, serv*ant*, coron*et*, cigar*ette*, gran*ary* ("grain-ary"), bak*er*, conduct*or*, east*ward*, clock*wise*, typ*ist*, duck*ling*, hill*ock*, fam*ous*.
3. *Find the Stranger* horseman Cavalier rider stable Cavalry
4. (a) Who or what lives in the following homes:
   igloo, house, monastery, fortress (animal), kraal, sett or set, lodge (animal), apiary, aviary, kennel, hutch, form?
   (b) Where do these live:
   convicts, soldiers, nuns, vicar, fox, bear, horse, wild rabbits, eagles, cows, otter, pig, squirrel?
5. Complete this table:

Clue	*Who or what*	*Where*
He hews coal	miner	colliery
She types letters	——	——
——	auctioneer	——
a wild animal	——	holt

6. What is the difference between a sentry, a century, a cent and a scent?
7. Write correctly:
   (i) Thc horsemen's sleeping-skins were (dry, tepid, damp) with (dew, due).
   (ii) May we (practice, practise) tonight or (not, knot)?
   (iii) Take these shoes to be (sold, soled) and (healed, heeled).
8. What is the gender (masculine, feminine, common or neuter) of:
   horsemen, horsewomen, riders, horses, reins, saddle?
9. (a) What do these "sound-words" mean: crash, scream, sigh, mutter, rumble, screech, boom, clang, tick, whizz, thunder?
   (b) What is likely to make each sound?
10. *Remember:* Thunder and *lightning* *lightening* or growing lighter
    Use the two words to complete these sentences:
    (i) The —— zigzagged across the night sky.
    (ii) —— someone's burden is a kind deed.
    (iii) We cannot go on —— the cart as there will soon be nothing left in it.
11. *Spelling* (a) envelopes, etc.: sta . . . . (b) usually weekly or monthly booklets: mag. . . . . . (c) near our neck: sho. . . . . s (d) twisting: wri. . . . . . (e) unlikely: imp. . . . . . . (f) on the back of our hands: . . .u. . les (g) a barrier: obs. . . . . (h) without a sound: noi. . . . . . (i) thinking hard: tho. . . . . . . (j) kind, liberal: gen. . . . .
12. Think of words which sound the same but which are spelt differently:
    Steppes, plain, wait, vain, flee, allowed, blue, reins, wrap, lesson.
    Give the meaning of your words.
13. Give the Comparative and Superlative degrees of: strange, small, big, blue, slim, pretty (like this: heavy, heavier, heaviest).
14. Use these adverbs in sentences: coolly, awkwardly, confidently, dangerously.
15. Put suitable nouns into these sentences:
    (i) I did not see the —— occur but I heard the loud —— of brakes, the ear-splitting —— and the —— of ——.
    (ii) The —— roared along the ——, —— pouring from its —— and the —— of its —— echoing off the ——.
16. Write correctly:
    (i) Between you and (me, I), I think he is guilty.
    (ii) Let (you and me, you and I, me and you, I and you) go together.
    (iii) (Who's, Whose) is this new book?

17. Use in sentences: twelve horsemen   flitting clouds   constant thunder
in vain   leather-covered shields   blue marks.

Find Out

1. Find what these words mean, then use one from each group in sentences:
   emerge, submerge, verge, merge   coolly, cruelly
   accompany, a company, companion, compartment
   stamping, trampling, tampering, tempering, temper, distemper, distress, stress
   wheeling, wailing, whaling, heeling, hailing, ailing.
2. Find the meaning of: pull someone's leg, on one's last legs, not a leg to stand on; a dark horse, flogging a dead horse, horse-play, horse-sense, changing horses in mid-stream, a clothes-horse, vaulting-horse, ride the high horse, put the cart before the horse, You can take a horse to the water but you cannot make it drink.
3. *Joy and Sorrow* Make a list of nouns connected with (a) *joy*, like happiness, birthday, glee (b) *sorrow*, like tears, accident, sadness.
4. *Horses* Find out about horses so that you can answer these questions:
   How is the height of horses measured? What are these: the Derby, the Grand National, M.F.H., a Suffolk Punch, a steeplechase, cavalry, mustangs, Shetland ponies, hunters, hacks, Arab horses, colts, fillies, foals?
   Why are these horses famous in fact and fiction: Black Bess, Bucephalus, Pegasus, the Wooden Horse of Troy?

Book List

Sons of the Steppe by Hans Baumann.
Black Beauty by Anna Sewell.
Big Tiger and Christian by Fritz Muhlenweg.
White Riders; Strangers to the Marsh; Killer Dog by Monica Edwards.
National Velvet by Enid Bagnold.
King of the Wind; Misty of Chincoteague by Marguerite Henry.
Snow Cloud, Stallion by Gerald Raftery.
Horses, Horses, Horses edited by Phyllis R. Fenner.
The Observer's Book of Horses and Ponies by R. S. Summerhayes.
The Young Rider Through the Ages by Dorothy M. Stuart.

20 *Practice Makes Perfect*

The sun was just emerging from the edge of the Steppe when the twelve horsemen unwrapped themselves from their sleeping-skins. The distant stamping of hooves had awakened them. Down in the plain they saw a whole crowd of flitting clouds flying in all directions, suddenly wheeling about and sometimes recoiling. It looked dangerous. The twelve horsemen nevertheless behaved as coolly as if the strange cloud game, which was accompanied by constant thunder, did not concern them in the least, and as if they had nothing to do but to wait and see if two small individual clouds would detach themselves from the dust storm raging around the *Ordo*.

The twelve horsemen waited in vain the whole day long.

The bigger clouds, too, were again and again swallowed up by green patches as the two little ones had been the day before. Then horses and horsemen emerged, every ten an *arban*, every hundred a *yagun*—and sometimes ten *yaguns* joined together, making a *guran*, and one *guran* attacked the other or detached itself to flee. It was Sorgan-Shira's school, in which many divisions of a thousand men each were manœuvring.

The riders guided their horses without reins, and only by the pressure of their legs and the shifting of their weight in the saddle. They used their hands to manipulate their bows and arrows, to pull in front of them the shields which hung on their backs, or in the case of close fighting, to grasp their clubs or daggers. They were allowed to wield their clubs only against the leather-covered shields, and the daggers with which they were thrusting were wooden ones without points. When arrows whizzed towards the horsemen in an attack they ducked behind their shields, and the horses which were hit tried to make off—yet there were only blue marks and no wounds. The arrows were blunt.

From *Sons of the Steppe* by Hans Baumann

Sons of the Steppe is about Mongol warriors of the Far East, 800 years ago.

Comprehension

A 1. Who awoke at sunrise?
2. What had awakened them?
3. How long did the twelve men wait?
4. (a) Whose school is mentioned? (b) What special kind of school was it?
5. For which three actions did the riders use their hands?
6. What kind of cover did their shields have?
7. Why were their weapons not dangerous?
8. What marked the horses harmlessly?
9. Why were thousands of horsemen attacking one another?
10. Explain: emerging, unwrapped themselves, hooves, dangerous, thunder, in vain, patches, weight, horsemen, in all directions, accompanied by constant thunder, guided, reins, shields.

B 1. Which word tells us that this took place in Russia?
2. What were the flitting clouds?
3. Which word describes the weather that morning: cloudy, thundery, stormy, sunny, cool?
4. The twelve horsemen are following two boys, having been ordered to see that they do not stray or come to harm.
   (a) What in the extract suggests this?
   (b) What does this bodyguard tell us about the boys?
5. An *ordo* was a town on wheels, people moving to another home.
   What is the connection between an ordo, Eastern caravans and Western Wagon Trains?
6. What were these: an arban, a yagun, a guran?
7. How many horsemen were there in a division?
8. Why did the riders not use reins?
9. Why was a storm raging round the Ordo?
10. Explain: sleeping-skins, the edge of the Steppe, suddenly wheeling about and sometimes recoiling, It looked dangerous, nevertheless behaved as coolly as if . . . . , did not concern them, two small individual clouds, the strange cloud game, manœuvring, to manipulate their bows and arrows, close fighting, wield their clubs, only blue marks.
    What do you think this means: swallowed up by green patches?

21 *The Strange Guest*

The man who came with the barrow told us the mail had set him down the morning before at the "Royal George"; that he had inquired what inns there were along the coast, and hearing ours well spoken of, I suppose, and described as lonely, had chosen it from the others for his place of residence. And that was all we could learn of our guest.

He was a very silent man by custom. All day he hung round the cove, or upon the cliffs, with a brass telescope; all evening he sat in the corner of the parlour next the fire, and drank rum and water very strong. Mostly he would not speak when spoken to; only look up sudden and fierce, and blow through his nose like a fog-horn; and we and the people who came about our house soon learned to let him be. Every day, when he came back from his stroll, he would ask if any seafaring men had gone by along the road. At first we thought it was the want of company of his own kind that made him ask this question; but at last we began to see he was desirous to avoid them. When a seaman put up at the "Admiral Benbow" (as now and then some did, making by the coast road for Bristol), he would look in at him through the curtained door before he entered the parlour; and he was always sure to be as silent as a mouse when any such was present.

For me, at least, there was no secret about the matter; for I was, in a way, a sharer in his alarms. He had taken me aside one day, and promised me a silver fourpenny on the first of every month if I would only keep my "weather-eye open for a seafaring man with one leg", and let him know the moment he appeared. Often enough, when the first of the month came round, and I applied to him for my wage, he would only blow through his nose at me, and stare me down; but before the week was out he was sure to think better of it, bring me my fourpenny piece, and repeat his orders to look out for "the seafaring man with one leg".

From *Treasure Island* by R. L. Stevenson

Comprehension

A 1. Where had the guest left the coach in which he had travelled?
2. What inquiry had he made there?
3. (a) Was he a quiet or a talkative man? (b) Which sentence tells us?
4. What did he do all day?
5. What question did he ask every day on his return to the inn?
6. (a) When did the boy receive money? (b) How much?
(c) Why was he given this money?
7. What did the stranger do when a sailor stayed at the inn?
8. (a) Did the man like to give away money? (b) How do you know?
9. Why do you think the man wanted to know if a one-legged sailor arrived?
10. Explain: residence, guest, cove, fog-horn, seafaring, put up at the "Admiral Benbow", the coast road to Bristol, curtained door.

B 1. What was the name of the inn where the boy lived?
2. Read the first sentence of the extract again, as far as the words "Royal George ". Who is the person referred to as "him"?
3. Give two reasons why the guest chose to stay at the "Admiral Benbow".
4. (a) Why do you think he "hung round the cove, or upon the cliffs, with a brass telescope"? (b) Why do people sometimes do this today?
5. Why did the innkeeper's family think at first that the man was lonely?
6. (a) In which part of England was the "Admiral Benbow"?
(b) How do you know?
7. (a) ". . . and he was always sure to be as silent as a mouse when any such was present". Who was "any such"?
(b) Why do you think the guest was silent then?
8. Why do you think the guest was "sure to think better of it" and give the boy fourpence "before the week was out"?
9. What is the difference between a telescope and binoculars?
10. Explain: the mail, his place of residence, by custom, parlour, blow through his nose like a foghorn, the people who came about our house soon learned to let him be, the want of company, desirous to avoid them, a sharer in his alarms, keep my weather-eye open, the first of the month, I applied to him.

21 Language

1. (a) What is a prefix? (b) What is a suffix? (c) What does the suffix mean in these words: otherwise, famous, glorious, movable, useful, beautiful?
   (d) Give two more words ending in each suffix in (c): -wise, -ous, -able, -ful.
2. Use in sentences: lightning, lightening.
3. CONCORD. This means agreement: singular goes with singular, plural with plural:

Wrong	*Right*
I like *these sort* of sweets.	I like *this sort* of sweets.
There *was many* people there.	There *were many* people there.
Both men *is writing* letters.	*Both* men *are writing* letters.

This sounds easy but mistakes are easily made. Which is correct: (i) or (ii)?

(i) Neither of the boys are to blame.

(ii) Neither of the boys is to blame.

Sentence *(ii)* is correct. *Neither* means the two boys separately, one at a time.

Remember: When there are several people or things but we are thinking about them separately, one at a time, the subject of the sentence (the "doer" of the action) and the verb are singular: *Each* of the three boys *has* paid *his* fare.

Here is a list of singular subjects or parts of subjects, like "each": none of, one of, either of, neither of, every one of, every, anybody, anyone, everyone, everybody, no one, nobody.

Write these correctly:

(i) Each of the boys (are, is) sorry and (is, are) going to apologise.

(ii) Everyone (was, were) happy at the result.

(iii) Neither John nor Harry (learn, learns) quickly.

(iv) None of the jockeys (was, were) ready for the race.

(v) I do not believe either of the mischievous boys (is, are) sorry for (their, his) bad behaviour.

4. ". . . blow through his nose like a foghorn. . . ."

Remember: like a foghorn BUT *as* a foghorn *blows* (NOT "like a foghorn blows").

Write correctly:

(i) Susan sews (like, as) her mother.

(ii) Susan sews (like, as) her mother does.

(iii) You are behaving (like, as) a very naughty child!

5. Think of words which sound exactly the same but which are spelt differently: guest, mail, told, ours, through, lightning, links, loan, made, main.
Give the meaning of your words.
6. What is the difference in meaning between: residence, residents; patience, patients; correspondence, correspondents; assistance, assistants?
7. *Find the Stranger* The "Royal George" The "Admiral Benbow" resident inn
8. *Spelling:* (a) people on a journey: tra....... (b) lift: ho... (c) like winter: win... (d) decided: res..... (e) lazy: ind..... (f) busy: ind........ (g) annoyed: ind...... (h) cannot be seen: inv...... (i) cannot be beaten: inv....... (j) revenge: ven......
9. "... bring me my fourpenny piece ..."
Say what is the difference in meaning between:
The guest said he would bring my fourpenny piece.
The guest said he would fetch my fourpenny piece.
Use "bring" and "fetch" in two sentences of your own.
10. Comment on these phrases from the Comprehension extract (any errors?):
look up sudden and fierce next the fire
11. Use *learn* and *teach* in sentences.
12. Give the plural of: man, guest, telescope, mouse, penny.
Give the singular of: cliffs, scissors, shelves, gases, solos, measles.
13. Insert the apostrophe and use in interesting sentences:
the mans barrow the guests telescope peoples opinions seamens visits
14. (a) What are the abbreviations for these counties: Gloucestershire, Durham, Bedfordshire, Hampshire, Nottinghamshire, Wiltshire, Lincolnshire?
(b) What are the complete words for these abbreviations: photo, gym, phone, plane, pram, radio-gram, piano, exam, bus, TV?
15. (a) Give the masculine of mistress, witch, widow, heiress, negress, abbess.
(b) Give the feminine of tiger, conductor, steward, son-in-law, nephew.
16. Think of ALL the meanings of barrow, mail, fire, company, present, blow, stamping, down, plain, club, vain, close.
17. Give the nouns, verbs and adverbs formed from these adjectives: beautiful, sharp, soft, bright, silent, dangerous; like this example: *adjective: sweet*
noun: sweetness verb: sweeten adverb: sweetly.
18. Use in sentences: "Royal George" along the coast lonely guest brass telescope curtained door strange as silent as a mouse.

Find Out

1. Find what these words mean, then use one from each group in sentences:
   admiral, admirable, admiration, admission, admonish, administer
   custom, accustom, customary, customer   royal, loyal, royalty, loyalty
   wages, salary, celery, celebrity, celebrated   barrow, burrow, borrow, lend
   treasure, pleasure, leisure, seizure   piece, peace, police, please, pleas.
2. Find the meaning of: grinning like a Cheshire cat, send to Coventry, speak broad Derbyshire, an Oxford accent, a Bath bun, Eccles cake, Bakewell tart, Swiss roll, Dundee cake, Madeira cake, Yorkshire pudding, Lincoln green, the Norfolk Broads, Cheddar Gorge, Cheshire (etc.) cheese, a Suffolk Punch.
3. *Buildings* (a) Find out the difference, if any, between: inn, hotel, tavern, public house, off-licence, boarding house, lodgings, guest house.
   (b) Do the same with these dwellings: cottage, palace, villa, detached house, semi-detached house, terraces, bungalow, flat, skyscraper, mansion, Hall, House, house, Home, home.
4. *Instruments* Make a list of instruments, not musical, and explain their use. Here are some: telescope, periscope, stethoscope, microscope, meter, thermometer, barometer, microphone, megaphone, telephone.

Book List

Treasure Island by Robert Louis Stevenson.
Adventures of Ben Gunn by R. F. Delderfield.
The Swiss Family Robinson by J. R. Wyss.
The Coral Island by R. M. Ballantyne.
Robinson Crusoe by Daniel Defoe.
Islands of Adventure by Ray Bethers.
Coconut Island by Robert Gibbings.
The Islanders by Roland Pertwee.
Crusoe Island by M. E. Atkinson.
The Treasure of the Isle of Mist by W. W. Tarn.
The Ann and Hope Mutiny by Christopher Webb.

Comprehension comes at the end of this exercise.

22 *Language*

1. Write correctly:
   (i) Each child (was, were) eager to make Murphy talk.
   (ii) None of the roads (was, were) safe.
   (iii) Everybody (is, are) delighted to be leaving Kullaroo.
   (iv) Murphy's hat and coat (was, were) worn out.
   (v) There (is, are) many people who would like to go to Australia.

2. COMPARATIVE AND SUPERLATIVE 2 ". . . the range ahead looked *larger*, *more solid*, and infinitely *higher* . . ."

   We saw in Exercise 14 the simple way of forming the Comparative and Superlative degrees of adjectives: larger, largest; higher, highest.

   Another way is to add *more* and *most*, instead of changing the ending to *er* or *est*: solid, more solid, most solid   more beautiful, most beautiful.

   We do this with adjectives which would sound awkward if we added *er* and *est*, especially long adjectives: *more beautiful*, *most beautiful* sound better.

   Adverbs: Adverbs are usually long words, so they usually take *more* and *most*: comfortably, more comfortably, most comfortably.

   Give the Comparative and Superlative of (a) these adjectives: delicious, splendid; and (b) these adverbs: splendidly, easily, carefully.

3. *Find the Stranger* creeks foothills plains hills town grass

4. Form adjectives from remark, distance, sincerity, fright, courtesy.

5. *Spelling* (a) make longer: len . . . . . (b) unbelievable: inc . . . . (c) wasting money: ext . . . . (d) disagreeing noisily: qua . . . . (e) proud: hau . . . . (f) happily: for . . . . (g) happening: occ . . . . . . (h) worry: anx . . . . (i) very large: im . . . . . (j) bravely: cou . . . .

6. What is the difference between these collections of trees: clump, copse, coppice, grove, wood, woodland, plantation, orchard, forest, jungle, spinney, thicket, avenue?

7. (a) What is the Future tense of: they bought their bread, Murphy started to talk, I rode in the back, we enjoyed, she is, Mike spoke?
   (b) Give the Simple Past tense of: He has gone out, dogs have bitten, Flowers have grown, I have seen, The monitor has rung the bell.

8. Choose from the words in brackets one word which is connected with the words at the beginning of the line, then say why you chose each word:
   (a) leopard, frog (Waterloo, kangaroo, bamboo, cuckoo)
   (b) cattle, sheep (bull, mare, king, goats, ewe, vixen)
   (c) flat, dusty (rain, rocky, view, skyline, miles)
   (d) bend, twist (straight, rigid, flexible, stiff)
   (e) blue, yellow (sky, sea, dust, crimson, dark, bright)
   (f) homestead, house (town, county, continent, cottage, street)
9. What are these places: nursery (2), menagerie, docks, quay, warehouse, factory, gas-works, colliery, university?
10. Think of words which sound exactly the same but which are spelt differently: mettle, meddle, bread, meat, hole, holy, creeks, maze, manner, mare.
    Give the meaning of your words.
11. What are the opposites of poverty, hills, enclosed, believe, over, occasional, foothills, smooth, health, courteous?
12. Write one word for each of these, beginning with the letter in brackets: (i) without grass (g) (ii) the skyline (h) (iii) not often (s) (iv) over and over again (r) (v) a person from abroad (f) (vi) impudent (i) (vii) inquisitive (c) (viii) meddle (i) (ix) not accidental (i) (x) can be seen through (t)
13. Use the following words in sentences, putting several into one sentence if you wish:
    (a) as nouns: stop, steering, talk, tackle, flat, progress.
    (b) as verbs: twist, bend, time, season, wheel, progress.
14. Add prefixes to these words, then say what their new meaning is: complete, earth, crossed, block, side, easily, cultivated, sphere, port.
    Some of the words will take more than one prefix, like "disarrange, rearrange".
15. What do these abbreviations mean: Salop., Oxon., Bucks., Staffs., Lancs.?
16. Who designs or plans new buildings, rides racehorses, attends to people's teeth, replaces broken window-panes, sells vegetables, sells tobacco and cigarettes, tests eyesight, carves statues, climbs high chimneys, etc., in order to repair them, types letters?
17. Write correctly:
    (i) i have been this way before murphy told us have you
    (ii) no we have not mick replied speaking for all of us
    (iii) then id better tell you something about this part of australia said murphy
    (iv) six and silver is the title of an australian story by joan phipson

18. Use in sentences: Kullaroo turning north a dim blue mass early spring treeless paddocks the shadeless plain rocky outcrops sign of life.

Find Out

1. Find what these words mean, then use one from each group in sentences:
   prospect, prospector, prosperous, prosperity Ranges, Rangers, strangers
   paddock, padlock, paddle, puddle, straddle, saddle protrude, intrude
   except, accept, affect, effect, infection, confectionery country, county.
2. Find the meaning of: to be yellow, yellow jack, a yellow-hammer; a bolt from the blue, look blue, Navy blue, a bluebottle, blue-jacket, the Blue Peter, a University Blue, ultramarine blue, once in a blue moon, Prussian blue, true blue, bluebells, blue blood, Light or Dark Blues; fade into the distance, keep one's distance, distance no object, Distance lends enchantment.
3. *Homes* Make two lists:
   (a) homes of humans, animals, birds, etc.
   (b) words containing *house*, like lighthouse and household, plus the meaning of each word.
4. *Australia* Find Australia in your atlas and on the globe, then find out what these are: aborigines, kangaroo, koala, dingo, cassowary, emu, kookaburra, the Royal Flying Doctor Service, N.S.W.

   What had Captain Cook and Tasman to do with Australia?

Book List

Six and Silver by Joan Phipson.
Doctor with Wings; The New Australians by Allan Aldous.
Bush Voyage by S. Fennimore.
Bush Christmas by Ralph Smart.
Adventure in the Outback by Phyllis M. Power.
Young Kangaroo by M. W. Brown.
Kangaroo Twins by Inez Hogan.
The Australian Twins by Daphne Rooke.
The Australia Book; Exploring Australia by Eve Pownall.
Kangaroo Coolaroo by L. S. Eliott.
By the Sandhills of Yamboorah by R. Ottley.

22 *North of Kullaroo*

They did not stop long in Kullaroo. They bought their bread and their meat, and set off again, turning north out of the town. In the distance ahead they could see the Karkoo Ranges, a dim blue mass on the sky-line. There had been little rain here in the early spring, and the country through which they travelled was flat and bare and dusty. The dirt road lay yellow and uninteresting before them, without a bend or a twist. From time to time they passed small, poverty-stricken homesteads, for the soil here, even in a good season, was poor. Occasionally in the treeless paddocks were groups of thin cattle. They did not see any sheep.

There was nothing in the immediate prospect to enliven them, but Murphy, once settled comfortably behind his steering wheel and with the town behind him, started to talk. At first he made only odd remarks, brief announcements of the names of creeks or properties, but by degrees he warmed up and began a flow of reminiscence and anecdote that kept them enthralled as the miles fell away. As he talked he gesticulated with his hands, and their progress became erratic and exciting. They noticed also (it was Mick, directly behind him, who pointed it out to the others) that with the years the top of his hat had worn a hole in the lining of the hood. It seemed only a matter of time before he would be driving with an entirely unobstructed view, his head protruding through the hood itself.

After a time they came to the end of the flat country. They were approaching the foothills and the range ahead looked larger, more solid, and infinitely higher. The shadeless plain gave way to timbered hills deep in grass and full of rocky outcrops. The road, as such, ended, and they passed on to a track through enclosed paddocks with many gates. As the old car wound its way deeper into the hills, bounding over boulders, concealed holes in the grass, and rocky creeks, it began to show its mettle. No well-bred motor-car would have tackled such a track.

From *Six and Silver* by Joan Phipson

Comprehension

A 1. What is Kullaroo?
2. Which two shops did the travellers probably visit?
3. What could they see in the distance: blue sky, mountains, mist, sea?
4. Why was the country bare and dusty?
5. What was the driver's name?
6. How do you know that they travelled a long way in the car?
7. (a) Who sat behind the driver? (b) What did he notice?
8. Where did the road end?
9. What were hidden in the grass?
10. Explain: dirt road, the skyline, the soil, occasionally, treeless, shadeless, a track, settled comfortably, steering wheel, only odd remarks, brief announcements, as the miles fell away.

B 1. Do the names Kullaroo and Karkoo suggest that this took place in a certain country? If so, which country and why?
2. In which direction were the mountains?
3. Give other words for (a) skyline (b) gesticulated with his hands (c) erratic (d) protruding (e) timbered hills.
4. What are (a) foothills (b) outcrops (c) creeks (d) plains (e) ranges?
5. (a) What time of year is it likely to be in this extract? (b) Why do you think so?
6. Why did the car begin to swerve?
7. ". . . it began to show its mettle." Explain this.
8. "No well-bred motor-car would have tackled such a track." Explain this.
9. How can you tell that the track through the "timbered hills" was not straight?
10. Explain, using your dictionary if you need help: poverty-stricken homesteads, treeless paddocks, enclosed paddocks, the immediate prospect, enliven them, properties, by degrees he warmed up, a flow of reminiscence and anecdote, kept them enthralled, their progress became erratic and exciting, directly behind him, only a matter of time, an entirely unobstructed view.

23 *A Summer Noon*

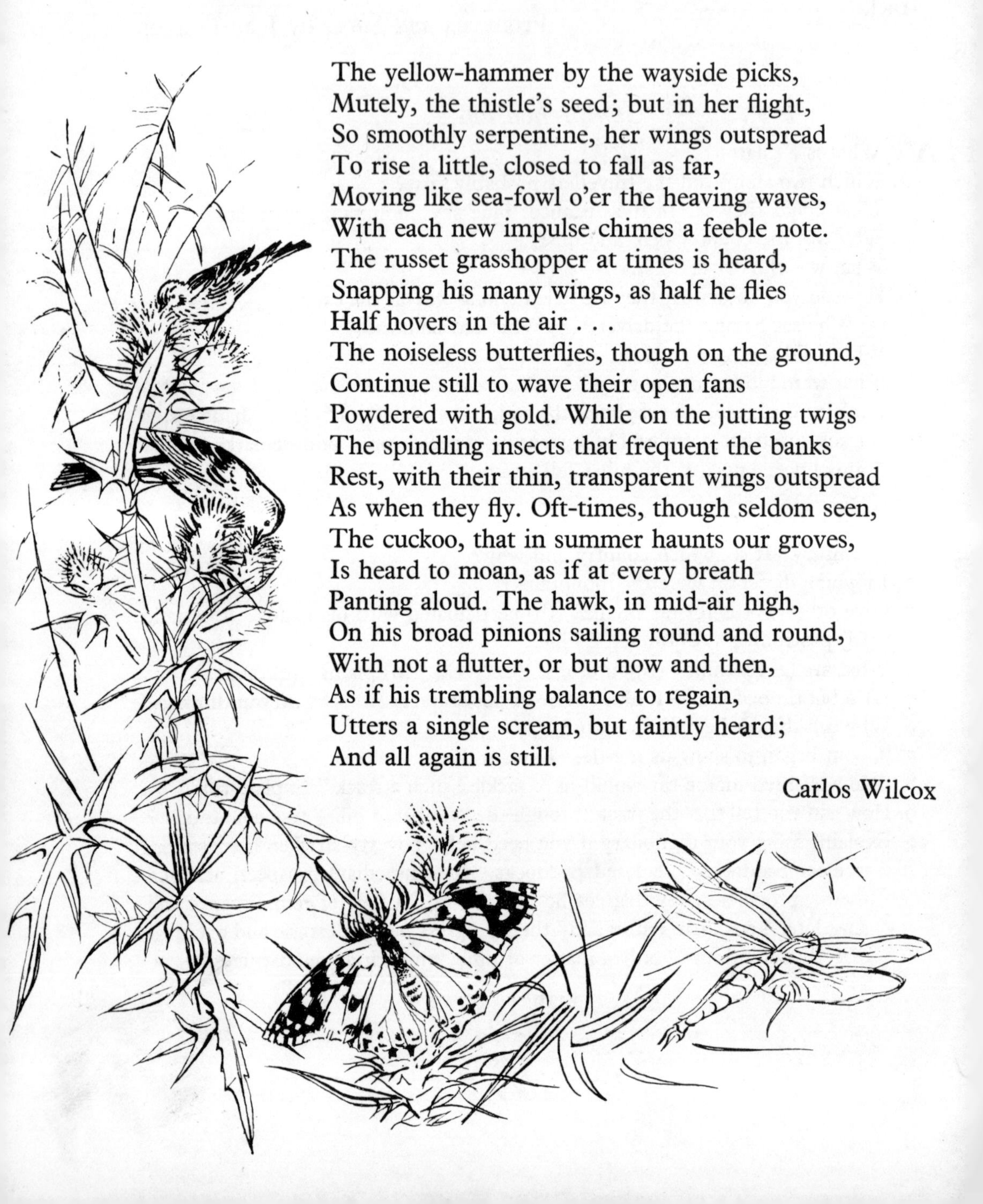

The yellow-hammer by the wayside picks,
Mutely, the thistle's seed; but in her flight,
So smoothly serpentine, her wings outspread
To rise a little, closed to fall as far,
Moving like sea-fowl o'er the heaving waves,
With each new impulse chimes a feeble note.
The russet grasshopper at times is heard,
Snapping his many wings, as half he flies
Half hovers in the air . . .
The noiseless butterflies, though on the ground,
Continue still to wave their open fans
Powdered with gold. While on the jutting twigs
The spindling insects that frequent the banks
Rest, with their thin, transparent wings outspread
As when they fly. Oft-times, though seldom seen,
The cuckoo, that in summer haunts our groves,
Is heard to moan, as if at every breath
Panting aloud. The hawk, in mid-air high,
On his broad pinions sailing round and round,
With not a flutter, or but now and then,
As if his trembling balance to regain,
Utters a single scream, but faintly heard;
And all again is still.

Carlos Wilcox

Comprehension

A 1. What is a yellow-hammer?

2. (a) Where is it? (b) What is it doing?
3. What is brownish-red in colour?
4. (a) What are silent? (b) What are they doing?
5. Where are the insects?
6. What moans?
7. What screams?
8. How many birds are mentioned?
9. Why do you think the hawk is flying round and round?
10. Explain: by the wayside, the thistle's seed, her flight, wings outspread, sea-fowl, heaving waves, chimes a feeble note, hovers, continue, seldom, broad pinions, sailing round and round, a single scream.

B 1. When is the yellow-hammer silent?

2. (a) How can her flight be "smoothly serpentine", if the suffix INE means "like"?
   (b) How does she use her wings to make her flight "smoothly serpentine"?
3. What have these to do with a "smoothly serpentine" flight:
   (a) "each new impulse" (line 6)
   (b) line 5?
4. Describe the grasshopper's flight.
5. Explain line 11.
6. (a) What do you think "spindling insects" are like? (b) What are they doing?
7. Are cuckoos (a) heard and seen (b) seen but not heard (c) heard but not seen (d) heard and sometimes seen (e) often heard but not often seen?
8. Describe the hawk's flight.
9. What in this poem (a) sings weakly (b) eats (c) has several wings (d) has gold-dusted wings?
10. Explain: picks mutely, snapping his many wings; as half he flies, half hovers; jutting twigs, frequent the banks; thin, transparent wings; haunts our groves, as when they fly, with not a flutter, his trembling balance to regain, utters.

23 Language

1. Give the Comparative and Superlative of (a) adjectives: famous, brilliant (b) adverbs: roughly, smoothly (c) far (2 Comparatives; 2 Superlatives).

   Give the exact meaning of (i) A further cry rent the air. (ii) A farther cry rent the air.

2. SUBJECT AND OBJECT "The yellow-hammer ...... picks ..... the thistle's seed." The action: picks.

   Who or what does the action? *What* picks? *The yellow-hammer.*

   Who or what has that action done to it? The yellow-hammer picks *what*? *The thistle's seed.*

   Remember: The one who does the action is called the SUBJECT.
   The one receiving the action is called the OBJECT.

   Longer subjects and objects:

   The rough boy kicked the blue ball. The rough boy: subject; the blue ball: object.

   (a) Pick out the subjects and objects:

   (i) The dog is eating its dinner.
   (ii) The russet grasshopper snaps its wings.
   (iii) Hawks chase sparrows.

   (b) *Remember* these pronouns which are often wrongly used:

Subject	*Object*
I	me
he	him
she	her
who	whom

   Remembering which are subjects and which are objects, use the correct pronouns in these sentences:

   (i) (He, Him) and (me, I) climbed wearily up the steep hill.
   (ii) (She, Her) and (I, me) picked the flowers.
   (iii) (Who, Whom) found the lost dog?
   (iv) (Whom, Who) did the police suspect?

3. *Find the Stranger* aloud seldom faintly feeble smoothly

4. Complete these: a punnet of ——, a skein of ——, an anthology of ——, a bale of ——, a tuft of ——, a flock of ——, a herd of ——, a shoal of ——.

5. "The spindling insects that frequent the banks"

   (a) What part of speech is "frequent"?

(b) Use "frequent" as an adjective.
(c) Is there any difference in pronunciation?
(d) Give a noun/verb which changes emphasis (or the way we say it) in the same way, like an *ob*ject/to ob*ject*.

6. Make sense out of these jumbled words:
   (a) cuckoo groves summer our haunts the in.
   (b) sails hawk and round round the air the in high.
   (c) noiseless butterflies are the.
   (d) of flight yellow-hammer serpentine smoothly is the the.

7. What are all the things in each group?
   cuckoo, hawk, yellow-hammer
   iron, steel, lead, copper
   cotton, wool, calico, silk
   coach, train, omnibus, liner
   barley, wheat, oats, rye
   Paris, Berlin, Tokio, Rome
   Ouse, Trent, Derwent, Humber

8. *Spelling* (a) all round it: sur . . . . . ing (b) friend: acq . . . . (c) people in church or chapel: con . . . . (d) opposite of loosening: tig . . . . (e) will float: buo . . . . (f) many: num . . . . . (g) in the Army: sol . . . . . (h) a sailing-boat: ya . . . (i) and (j) cannot be avoided: una . . . . or ine . . . .

9. Note that there are no rhymes in the poem "A Summer Noon".
   This is called Blank Verse.
   Think of words which rhyme with these words but which end in a different spelling, like break, cake: route, seize, grey, hail, buoy, grief.

10. Think of opposites: at times, continue, seldom, a single, transparent, noiseless, feeble, broad, thin, faintly, still, mutely, rise, closed.

11. (a) What does the prefix mean in these words: anti-aircraft gun, anteroom, contradict, export, import, interrupt, vice-captain?
    (b) Give a prefix to these words, then explain their new meaning: press, biography, agree, noon, capable, national, take, pare, turn, safe.

12. (a) Give the masculine of: bride, doe, filly, duck, goose, ewe, hind, landlady, nun, peahen, mare, aunt.
    (b) Give the feminine of: actor, conductor, dog, duke, fox, heir, hero, host, manager, nephew, prince, bachelor.

13. Using your dictionary if necessary, give the meaning of these words: punctual, efficient, tempestuous, tendency, obstinacy, dejected, moderate, pronounce.

14. Which creatures screech, twitter, gobble, warble, chirp, coo, scream, gibber, bray, grunt, roar, low, whinny, neigh, purr?
15. Usc in sentences: (i) confide (ii) confidence (iii) confident (iv) confidently. Say which part of speech each of those words is.
16. Use in sentences: summer noon serpentine heaving waves a feeble note hovers powdered with gold jutting twigs a single scream.

Find Out

1. Find what these words mean, then use one from each group in sentences:
   russet, rusty, rustic, rustle, bustle   pinions, to pinion, opinion
   haunts, haughty, naughty, draughty, draughtsman, draughts   groves, grieves
   a yellow-hammer, a yellow hammer   outspread, outskirts, outwit, outsider.
2. Find the meaning of: take wing, on the wing, take under one's wing, a hospital wing, to wing, clip someone's wings; hawk-eyed, hawk-nosed, to hawk, a hawker; to kill two birds with one stone, a bird's eye view, The early bird catches the worm. Birds of a feather flock together. The bird has flown. A bird in hand is worth two in the bush.
3. *Fear* Make a list of words connected with fear, like scream, terror, nightmare. Give the meaning of your words.
4. *Birds of Prey* Make a list of birds of prey like the sparrow-hawk, kestrel and jay. What are eaglets, eyries, tiercels, peregrine falcons, "wind-hovers", kites, choughs, hobbies, harriers, bowets, falconry, an eyas?

List of Poems

A Summer Noon by Carlos Wilcox.
The Thrush's Nest; The Yellowhammer by John Clare.
The Reverie of Poor Susan; After the Storm by William Wordsworth.
The Thrush's Song by W. Macgillivray.
The Jackdaw by William Cowper.
Stormcock in Elder by Ruth Pitter.
Follow! Follow! Follow! by James Stephens.
The Ecstatic by C. Day Lewis.
Humming-Bird by D. H. Lawrence.
The Water-Ousel by Mary Webb.

Comprehension comes at the end of this exercise.

24 *Language*

1. (a) Which of these pronouns can be used as subjects of sentences and which as objects: who, he, we, whom, them, I?
   (b) Make a list of the subjects and a list of the objects:
      (i) The king scolded the lazy servant.
      (ii) The young girl rode a small, quiet pony.
2. ABBREVIATIONS "The Ascent of Everest": Mount Everest: Mt. Everest. So far we have put a full stop to show abbreviations, like Mt., St., Rd., etc. You will find, however, that many people follow the advice of the best-known English Language reference book* and omit the full stop after an abbreviation which has the *first* and *last* letters of the full word, like *Mt: Mount*, *Mr: Mister*, *Dr: Doctor*. Abbreviations which do not do this, like Capt. for Captain, Rev. for Reverend, Prof. for Professor, etc., still keep the full stop.
   (a) What do these abbreviations mean, all of which follow a person's name: B.A. B.Sc. M.A. M.Sc. M.P. V.C. M.M. D.F.C. D.S.O. D.S.C.?
   (b) What do these mean: P.C. S.S. H.M.S. O.H.M.S. B.B.C. I.T.V. A.T.V. P.T.O. R.S.V.P. (why?) B.O.A.C. B.E.A. G.C.E. Esq. (meaning and use) C.O.D. (use?) B.C. A.D. a.m. p.m. ?
3. Put into Direct Speech: Sir Edmund Hillary said that he enjoyed the climb as much as he had ever enjoyed a fine climb in his own country.
4. "The *Ascent* of Everest". Do not confuse *ascent* (the noun) and *ascend* (the verb); *descent* (the noun) and *descend* (the verb).
   Write four sentences, using these four words correctly.
5. Which of these proverbs fits the Comprehension extract, "Climbing Everest"?
   Too many cooks spoil the broth. More haste, less speed.
   The early bird catches the worm. Where there's a will, there's a way.
6. What do we call these workers: (i) fruit-seller (ii) racehorse-rider (iii) burst-pipe-repairer (iv) rabbit-stealer (v) suit-maker (vi) docks-worker (vii) drum-player (viii) luggage-carrier at stations?
7. (a) Give the plural of: I, he, me, to her, his coat, my house, your friend.

* H. W. Fowler: "Modern English Usage."

(b) Change into the singular:

Both climbers were exhausted and could not reach the ropes thrown down by the rescue-teams.

8. (a) Write in the present tense:

The weather was perfect. We knew about the rock step. I sank their spikes into the frozen snow.

(b) Change to the past tense (Simple Past: ran, swam, spoke, etc.):

The climbers will fight their way up the mountain, bring supplies to us and encourage us to try again.

(c) Write in the future tense:

The postbox was not cleared on Christmas Day.

9. Write another word at the end of each set in order to complete it:

(a) five, ten, twenty, ——. (b) icy, cold, warm, hot, ——.
(c) second, minute, hour, day, ——.
(d) Sunday, Tuesday, Thursday, ——. (e) January, April, July, ——.

10. Write these sentences (or their letters a, b, c, d, e) in their proper order:

(a) They cheered when they reached the summit.
(b) The weather looked promising when they started out.
(c) The final section was surprisingly easy.
(d) They tackled the mountain with confidence.
(e) Slowly and steadily they climbed, refusing to be dismayed by unexpected difficulties and hazards.

11. *Find the Stranger* smooth hastily interesting feeble holdless

12. Say what parts of speech these words are: a *perfect* day, the discomfort, removed, closely, by, I, but, Oh!

13. *Spelling* (a) cannot be penetrated: imp........ (b) offer to do it: vol...... (c) show how to do it: dem........ (d) gave a sign: sig...... (e) one who inspects: ins...... (f) does party tricks: con..... (g) to wave: bra..... (h) a trip: jou.... (i) alarmed: anx.... (j) obvious, cannot be hidden: con........

14. Give the opposite of perfect, discomfort, cold, backwards, attached, difficult, *bitter* wind, *bitter* medicine, hastily, enjoy.

15. Think of words which sound exactly the same but which are spelt differently: martial, maze, meet, medal, metal, might, miner, missed, moan, morning. Give the meaning of your words.

16. Precaution, predict, preface, prefer, prehistoric, prepare.
    (a) What does the prefix mean? (b) What do the words mean? (c) Use them in six sentences.
17. (a) Who or what live in prisons, barracks, warrens, holts, dreys, lairs, orphanages, byres?
    (b) What are the homes of badgers, moles, foxes, eagles, budgerigars, horses?
18. Use in sentences: on one occasion a difficult section blinded the bitter wind hastily aerial photographs binoculars fortunately.

Find Out

1. Find what these words mean, then use one from each group in sentences: ascent, assent, consent, ascend, descend, descent, descendant, precedent, president perfect, prefect, perforated, prefabricated, preferred, conferred, referred photographs, autographs, graphs barrier, harrier, farrier, carrier.
2. Find the meaning of: on bended knee, brought to their knees, knee-cap, knee-deep, shoulder a burden, put one's shoulder to the wheel (why?), broad-shouldered, cold-shoulder someone, fire-arms, the arm of the law, take up or lay down arms, keep at arm's length, welcome with open arms, To Arms!, armed, armada, armadillo, unarmed, unharmed.
3. *Actions* Make a list of actions, like mountaineering, skating, camping, trespassing, persevering. Give the meaning of the words.
4. *Mount Everest* Find out all you can about Mount Everest.
   Explain the connection between Mount Everest and Sherpas, Nepal, 29,002, Sir George Everest, Mallory, Eric Shipton, 1953, Sir John Hunt, Hillary and Tenzing.

Book List

The Ascent of Everest; Our Everest Adventure by Sir John Hunt.
Man of Everest by J. R. Ullman.
Men Against Everest by Howard Marshall.
The Epics of Everest by Leonard Wibberley.
The True Book about Everest by Eric Shipton.
The Picture of Everest by Alfred Gregory.
Volcano Adventure by Willard Price.
Kami the Sherpa by Showell Styles.

24 *Climbing Everest*

The weather for Everest seemed practically perfect. Insulated as we were in all our down clothing and windproofs, we suffered no discomfort from cold or wind. However, on one occasion I removed my sunglasses to examine more closely a difficult section of the ridge but was very soon blinded by the fine snow driven by the bitter wind and hastily replaced them. I went on cutting steps. To my surprise I was enjoying the climb as much as I had ever enjoyed a fine ridge in my own New Zealand Alps.

After an hour's steady going we reached the foot of the most formidable-looking problem on the ridge—a rock step some forty feet high. We had known of the existence of this step from aerial photographs and had also seen it through our binoculars from Thyangboche. We realized that at this altitude it might well spell the difference between success and failure.

The rock itself, smooth and almost holdless, might have been an interesting Sunday afternoon problem to a group of expert rock climbers in the Lake District, but here it was a barrier beyond our feeble strength to overcome. I could see no way of turning it on the steep rock bluff on the west, but fortunately another possibility of tackling it still remained. On its east side was another great cornice, and running up the full forty feet of the step was a narrow crack between the cornice and the rock. Leaving Tenzing to belay me as best he could, I jammed my way into this crack, then kicking backwards with my crampons I sank their spikes deep into the frozen snow behind me and levered myself off the ground. Taking advantage of every little rock hold and all the force of knee, shoulder and arms I could muster, I literally cramponed backwards up the crack, with a fervent prayer that the cornice would remain attached to the rock.

From *The Ascent of Everest* by Sir John Hunt
Chapter 16 *The Summit* by Sir Edmund Hillary

Comprehension

A 1. What is Everest?

2. (a) Did the cold wind worry the climbers? (b) How?
3. What were two reasons for wearing sunglasses?
4. (a) Why did one climber take off his sunglasses?
   (b) Why did he put them on again?
5. How long did it take them to reach the rock step?
6. Were the climbers strong or weak? Which words tell you?
7. What is Thyangboche?
8. (a) Were these men climbing on a Sunday afternoon?
   (b) Why is Sunday mentioned?
9. What were the names of the two climbers?
10. Explain: down clothing and windproofs, discomfort, the ridge, fine snow, feeble, a barrier, jammed my way into this crack, on one occasion, section, hastily replaced them, Alps, steady going, problem, crampons.

B 1. Why is "a group of expert rock climbers in the Lake District" mentioned?

2. (a) Who is the person "I" in the extract?
   (b) What is his nationality?
3. (a) Were the climbers surprised to find a high rock step barrier?
   (b) How do you know?
4. What was the problem they had to solve?
5. What do you think altitude (height) had to do with success or failure?
6. How did they overcome the barrier?
7. How do you think the other climber did this: "belay me"?
8. Can you tell, from the section beginning "On its east side" to the end of the extract, the answer to this: What is a cornice?
9. What did the climber fear might happen while he was cramponing backwards?
10. Explain: we suffered no discomfort, sunglasses, a difficult section, blinded by the fine snow, cutting steps, the most formidable-looking problem, binoculars, spell the difference, almost holdless, expert, levered myself.

Find out what aerial photographs are and the meaning of "insulated".

25 Escaping

The Stammgericht was a stew made from swedes, potatoes and carrots, but no meat. It was a generous helping, filling and warm. They had two more of the weak German beers and felt more full than they had felt since they had escaped. With a full stomach came renewed confidence.

"What do we do now?" John asked.

"Better not stay here. Let's walk round the town."

But it was worse in the street. Everyone seems to have something to do except us, Peter thought. This is going to be the worst part of the whole show, this trying to look inconspicuous with nothing to do. They tried looking into shop windows; but all the time the feeling of being watched grew more acute.

"I hate this town," John said. "Let's get out of it."

"No—we mustn't catch a train until it's dark. We've got to stay here until it's dark."

"We've got to do something."

"Let's look at this objectively," Peter said. "What should we do in England if we had a few hours to waste?"

"Go to the public library or a museum."

"Or to the cinema. Why not go to the cinema?"

John grinned. "We escape from a prison camp and the first afternoon out we go to the pictures."

"It'll be safer than the streets," Peter said.

They walked towards the cinema, feeling better now that they were doing something, and less conspicuous. There was a queue, and they joined it. The queue was mostly children, with a few women, an old man and some soldiers. They were the only young men in civilian clothes. They stood at the end of the queue hoping that no one would talk to them.

From *The Wooden Horse* by Eric Williams

Comprehension

A 1. What are the men's names?
2. What has happened before the extract begins?
3. (a) Who asked a question? (b) What was the answer?
4. What did they do first, so as not to attract attention in the street?
5. (a) Was someone watching them? (b) Why do you think that?
6. (a) Who did not like the town? (b) Can you think why he did not like it?
7. To which places would they go in England, if they had nothing to do?
8. (a) Did they walk straight into the cinema? (b) How do you know?
9. Why did they hope no one would talk to them?
10. Explain: stew, swedes, generous, filling, library, museum, queue, the whole show, a few hours to waste, cinema.

B 1. Complete this sentence by using one of the words or phrases in the brackets: The two men were (terrified, on holiday, in danger, sightseeing).
2. They had been in a prison-camp. Can you say why?
3. (a) What is "Stammgericht"? (b) Describe it. (c) Why has it such a strange name? (d) Can you think of a special reason why it was meatless?
4. (a) In which country do you think this happened? (b) Why do you think so? (c) Why might a clue *mislead* you?
5. (a) Which two sentences in the last paragraph suggest that this happened in wartime? (b) How do they suggest it?
6. Why would it be safer in a cinema?
7. Why do you think they did not go to the railway station in daylight?
8. Why did John think that going to the cinema was a joke?
9. (a) Which man is steadier than the other, more confident and obviously the "leader" in this escape? (b) How can you tell?
10. Explain: a generous helping, With a full stomach came renewed confidence, trying to look inconspicuous, the feeling of being watched grew more acute, less conspicuous, civilian clothes.

Find out the meaning of "Let's look at this objectively."

25

Language

1. What do these abbreviations mean: J.P. R.S.V.P. anon. O.H.M.S. R.A.F. Rev. M.F.H. & Co. Ltd. G.P.O. A.A. R.A.C. B.R.?

2. PROVERBS What is a proverb?

   Remember: Proverbs usually have a much wider meaning than the one given by the words themselves: "Make hay while the sun shines" means "Do something while you have the chance" and has nothing to do with haymaking.

   (a) When might you use that proverb?

   (b) Say what these proverbs mean and when you might use them:
   All's well that ends well. More haste, less speed. No news is good news.

   (c) Use a proverb in a sentence.

3. (a) Find five buildings mentioned in the Comprehension extract.

   (b) Where did the two men probably have their meal?

   (c) What is the difference between:
   (i) a church, chapel, cathedral, monastery, nunnery and convent?
   (ii) a cinema, a theatre, an operating theatre and a concert hall?
   (iii) an airport, an aerodrome and hangars?

   (d) ". . . the first afternoon out we go to the *pictures.*"
   Pictures hang on walls, in Art Galleries, etc. Put a better word in the quotation from "The Wooden Horse".

4. "weak German beers"

   What are the adjectives or nationalities of these countries: Austria, Australia, Belgium, Canada, China, Czechoslovakia, Egypt, England, Scotland, Ireland, Wales, France, Holland, Japan, Norway, Sweden, Portugal, Spain, Switzerland, Great Britain?

5. "They tried *looking* into shop windows. . . ."

   (a) What would it mean if we changed *looking* to (i) peeping (ii) peering (iii) staring?

   (b) What is the difference between watching, observing, noticing, spying, gazing?

6. *Find the Stranger* library museum prison cinema theatre

7. (a) Form adjectives from *confidence*, *hate*, *England* and use them in sentences.

   (b) Use in sentences the verb and noun *object*: to object, an object.

8. *Spelling* (a) release, disentangle: ext . . . . . . (b) slow in leaving: lin . . . . . . (c) make it seem more than it is: exa. . . . . . . (d) before winter: a. . . . .

(e) opposite of folly: wis... (f) tiresome: ted.... (g) in charge of a library: lib...... (h) height: alt..... (i) stonework: mas.... (j) sank: subs....

9. Think of words which sound exactly the same but which are spelt differently: muscle, need, new, night, nose, owed, pale, pain, pair, past.
Give the meaning of your words.

10. Change to Indirect Speech:
 (i) "What do we do now?" John asked.
 (ii) "We'd better not stay here," replied Peter. "Let's walk round the town."

11. Change to Direct Speech:
Peter told John that it would be unwise to go to the station before nightfall. John disagreed. Peter said angrily that he thought John was stupid.

12. Think of ALL the meanings of helping, felt, round, show, watch, train, safe, pound, match, hand, collier, bridge.

13. Put into alphabetical order: stew, carrots, grin, swede, generous, warm, confidence, weak, worse, street, window, say, cinema, queue.

14. Explain the meaning of these sentences:
 (i) The rebels were soon brought to their knees.
 (ii) If we all put our shoulders to the wheel, the job will soon be done.
 (iii) As I doubted the man's sincerity, I kept him at arm's length.

15. Give the meaning of these verbs: gnaw, gobble, devour, graze, gulp down, bolt, munch, chew.

16. Write correctly:
 (i) He (rung, rang) the door-bell, then (run, ran) away.
 (ii) They (sung, sang) carols in the Market Square.
 (ii) "He (doesn't, don't) know (anything, nothing) about our plan," said John.
 (iv) Mother has just (broke, broken) a (knew, new) plate.

17. Write correctly:
they went to the gaumont cinema as they were hours too early for the royal scot express to scotland the film was the wooden horse

18. What are similes? Give an example.

19. Use in sentences: swedes, potatoes and carrots renewed confidence the worst part inconspicuous shop windows the public library or a museum prison camp the end of the queue.

Find Out

1. Find what these words mean, then use one from each group in sentences:
   swedes, Swedes, tweed, Tweed, weeds   wooden, woollen
   confidence, confidential, confide, confine, confirm, confiscate, conflagration
   queue, quest, question, request, inquest, conquest, bequest
   generous, generosity, general, colonel, kernel.
2. Find the meaning of: go window-shopping, talk shop; look daggers, look blue, look for trouble, look after, look down on, look sharp, look up to someone, look up in a book, look through someone, look death in the face, Don't look a gift horse in the mouth. (explain) Look before you leap.
3. *Places* Make a list of buildings and places, especially rather unusual ones like a cul-de-sac, mews, a fly-over, an amphitheatre. Describe each one.
4. *Famous Escapes* Find out about famous escapes, like those by Bonnie Prince Charlie, Charles II, Jack Sheppard, Napoleon; also escapes in fiction.
   What is the connection between the following and escapes: Dunkirk 1940, Newgate Prison, Flora Macdonald, the Boscobel Oak, "The Wooden Horse", Monte Cristo?

Book List

The Wooden Horse by Eric Williams (abridged).
The Great Escape by Paul Brickhill (adapted by James Britton).
The True Book about Famous Escapes by Leonard Gribble.
Aztec Gold; Dauntless in Danger by Peter Dawlish.
Swallows and Amazons by Arthur Ransome.
The Cave by Richard Church.
The Pirates in the Deep Green Sea by Eric Linklater.
Kidnapped; The Black Arrow by Robert Louis Stevenson.
The Otterbury Incident by C. Day Lewis.
The Dark Lantern by V. Bayley.
Fighting Men by Henry Treece and E. Oakeshott.

Comprehension comes at the end of this exercise.

26 *Language*

1. Give the meaning of these proverbs: (i) A bad workman blames his tools. (ii) A drowning man will clutch at a straw. (iii) A stitch in time saves nine.
2. SIMILES If we say that someone is "as brown as a berry", we are saying that the person's colour is like, or SIMILAR to, a brown berry.

   Say why these expressions are vivid and interesting:

   The gardener was *as busy as a bee.*

   The thief was *as cunning as a fox.*

   The wicketkeeper was *as quick as lightning.*

   Remember: "as —— as ——": *similes*, describing in an interesting way.

   (a) Make similes from these words: deep (as deep as the ocean), straight, heavy, pretty, thin, flat, thick, light, tender, good, warm, white.

   (b) Complete these similes: as —— as water or a kitten, as —— as an owl or Solomon, as — as a lion, as —— as a bat, as —— as a lark.
3. *Find the Stranger* journey traveller trip voyage tour
4. *More about Concord or Agreement*. See Exercise 21.

   Remember: singular with singular; plural with plural.

   Be careful with sentences like these:

   (i) The wild rabbit, with many tame ones, *was* on show.

   (ii) Either the man or his wife *has* signed this form.

   Prove that they are correct like this:

   (i) The wild rabbit *was* on show, with many tame ones.

   (ii) Either the man *has* signed this form, or his wife *has* signed it.

   Write correctly:

   (a) The boy, with several girls, (was, were) late for school.

   (b) Ann, as well as Margaret, (is, are) always out early.

   (c) John and several other boys (was, were) late for school.
5. *Spelling* (a) one's home: res...... (b) picture and sound: tel....... (c) ferociously: f....... (d) letter-writing: cor........nce (e) measures temperature: ther....... (f) clever and capable: eff...... (g) like a mule: obs...... (h) nearly: prac....... (i) a lonely place: sol..... (j) unpleasant, obnoxious: obj.........

6. What is the difference in meaning between the two adjectives *considerable* and *considerate*? Use them in two sentences.

7. Think of words which sound exactly the same but which are spelt differently: sewed, forth, by, which, more, paws, peace, peal, pear, peer.
   Give the meaning of your words.

8. ". . . in such immense seas as Lake Superior. . . ."
   What is the difference, if any, between a lake, mere, tarn (see Exercise 29), pool, loch, lough, llyn, pond, lagoon, reservoir?

9. ". . . the inland *craft* of the fur-traders . . ."
   Give other meanings of *craft*, including words containing *craft*.
   Use one of the words in a sentence.

10. Choose the correct word in the brackets:
    (a) The careless boy is always asking if he may (borrow, lend) my rubber.
    (b) When you return, will you (fetch, bring, bought, brought) my case, please?
    (c) I looked through the (catalog, colleague, catalogue) to try to find a good but cheap tent.
    (d) The stone rolled slowly into the (cavalry, cavity, cavalier, cavalcade).
    (e) The disease was highly (infectious, inferior, infinite, infamous).

11. What are the *adjectives* formed from: anxiety, extent, probability; the *nouns* from buoyant, warm, splendid; the *verbs* from consultation, extent; the *adverbs* from severe, considerable?

12. Use these conjunctions in short sentences: if, until, after, because.

13. Put pronouns into these sentences:
    (i) —— broke this window?
    (ii) To —— did you give the letter?
    (iii) This is the man —— is going to referee our match.
    (iv) I found an old book —— was printed over a hundred years ago.
    (v) We lost —— dog but a farmer found —— in —— wood. —— had hurt —— back legs.

14. Think of better words for "got" in these short sentences: I got up early. I got out of bed. I got washed. I got dressed. I got my breakfast. My mother got my breakfast. I got my satchel. I got the bus to school. I got there late.

15. What are phrases, sentences and paragraphs? Give examples of the first two.

16. What is each of these: lighthouse, out-house, greenhouse, hot-house, bakehouse, farmhouse, public house, warehouse, houseboat, housekeeper, household?

17. (a) Give the plural of thief, lake, finch, country, day, army, wolf, leaf, he, I.
    (b) Give the singular of men, canoes, sheep, guides, sheaves, us, their, flies.
18. Give the masculine, feminine and young of sheep, deer, cats, tigers, goats, ducks.
19. Use in sentences: a deep bay   straight across   fourteen miles   severe storm   bark canoes   thin flat slips of wood   guides   anxiety.

Find Out

1. Find what these words mean, then use one from each group in sentences:
   point, pointless, point-duty, compass-points, poignant, pointed, pointer
   immense, immerse, imminent, eminent, permanent, prominent, promontory
   superior, inferior, interior, exterior, exit, entrance, entranced   courage, enrage.
2. Find the meaning of: a windcheater, get wind of something, sound in wind and limb, something in the wind, take the wind out of his sails, throw caution to the winds, a windbag, windfall, wind-gauge, wind-hover, windmill, wind-instruments, wind-jammer, see which way the wind blows, It's an ill wind which blows nobody any good.
3. *Similes* Make a list of similes, especially interesting ones like "as poor as a church-mouse" (why?), then say what each one might describe.
4. *Canada* Find Canada in your atlas and on the globe, then find out the answers to these questions:
   (a) What are these: C.P.R., R.C.M.P., the Rockies, Alberta, Saskatchewan, lumberjacks, prairies, Douglas Fir, the 49th Parallel?
   (b) What had these men to do with Canada: Wolfe, Montcalm, the Cabots, Hudson, Mackenzie, Vancouver?

Book List

The Young Fur-Traders by R. M. Ballantyne.
Man from St. Malo by R. D. Ferguson.
Frontenac and the Iroquois by Fred Swayze.
The Forest is my Kingdom by Janet Carruthers.
Lost in the Barrens by Farley Mowat.
White Fang by Jack London.
The Splendid Journey by Honoré Morrow.
Wild Life in Canada by C. B. Rutley.

26 *Crossing the Lake*

At this part of the lake there occurs a deep bay or inlet, to save rounding which travellers usually strike straight across from point to point, making what is called in *voyageur* parlance a *traverse*. These *traverses* are subjects of considerable anxiety, and frequently of delay to travellers, being sometimes of considerable extent, varying from four and five—and, in such immense seas as Lake Superior—to fourteen miles.

With boats, indeed, there is little to fear, as the inland craft of the fur traders can stand a heavy sea, and often ride out a pretty severe storm; but it is far otherwise with the bark canoes that are often used in travelling. These frail craft can stand very little sea—their frames being made of thin flat slips of wood and sheets of bark, not more than a quarter of an inch thick, which are sewed together with the fibrous roots of the pine (called by the natives *wattape*), and rendered water-tight by means of melted gum. Although light and buoyant, therefore, and extremely useful in a country where *portages* are numerous, they require very tender usage; and when a *traverse* has to be made, the guides have always a grave consultation with some of the most sagacious among the men, as to the probability of the wind rising or falling—consultations which are more or less marked by anxiety and tediousness in proportion to the length of the *traverse*, the state of the weather, and the courage or timidity of the guides.

On the present occasion there was no consultation, as has been seen. The *traverse* was a short one, the morning fine, and the boats good. A warm glow began to overspread the horizon, giving promise of a splendid day, as the numerous oars dipped with a plash and a loud hiss into the water, and sent the boats leaping forth upon the white waves.

From *The Young Fur-Traders* by R. M. Ballantyne

a voyageur: a boatman.

Comprehension

A 1. What is "a deep bay or inlet" on a lake?
2. (a) Which are safer in rough water: boats or canoes? (b) Why?
3. (a) What are canoe-frames made of? (b) How thick is this?
4. What is wattape?
5. Why is gum used in canoe-making?
6. What was the weather like on the day described in the extract?
7. (a) What was the "warm glow"? (b) What time of day was it?
8. How can you tell that there were many rowers?
9. Explain: "These frail craft can stand very little sea."
10. Explain: there occurs, straight across, anxiety, frequently, delay, travellers, varying, a pretty severe storm, it is far otherwise, bark canoes, sheets of bark, sewed together, courage.

B 1. Draw a bay or inlet in a lake and mark a "traverse" on it.
2. Why did a *traverse* worry and delay travellers?
3. Describe how a bark canoe was made.
4. We are told that bark canoes are "light and buoyant, therefore, and extremely useful in a country where *portages* are numerous . . ."
From this and our words *porter* and *transport*, what do you think *portages* were?
5. Why did guides usually have a discussion?
6. Which three facts increased the weariness and worry of these discussions?
7. Why were the guides in this story not worried about the traverse?
8. (a) What "require very tender usage"? (b) Why?
9. Find the words in the passage which mean: sage, wise; a long and tiresome time; able to float; a large number; solemn and serious.
10. Explain: to save rounding, from point to point, in voyageur parlance (*parlance:* a way of speaking), subjects, considerable extent, such immense seas, inland craft, heavy sea, frail craft, fibrous roots, rendered water-tight, grave consultation.

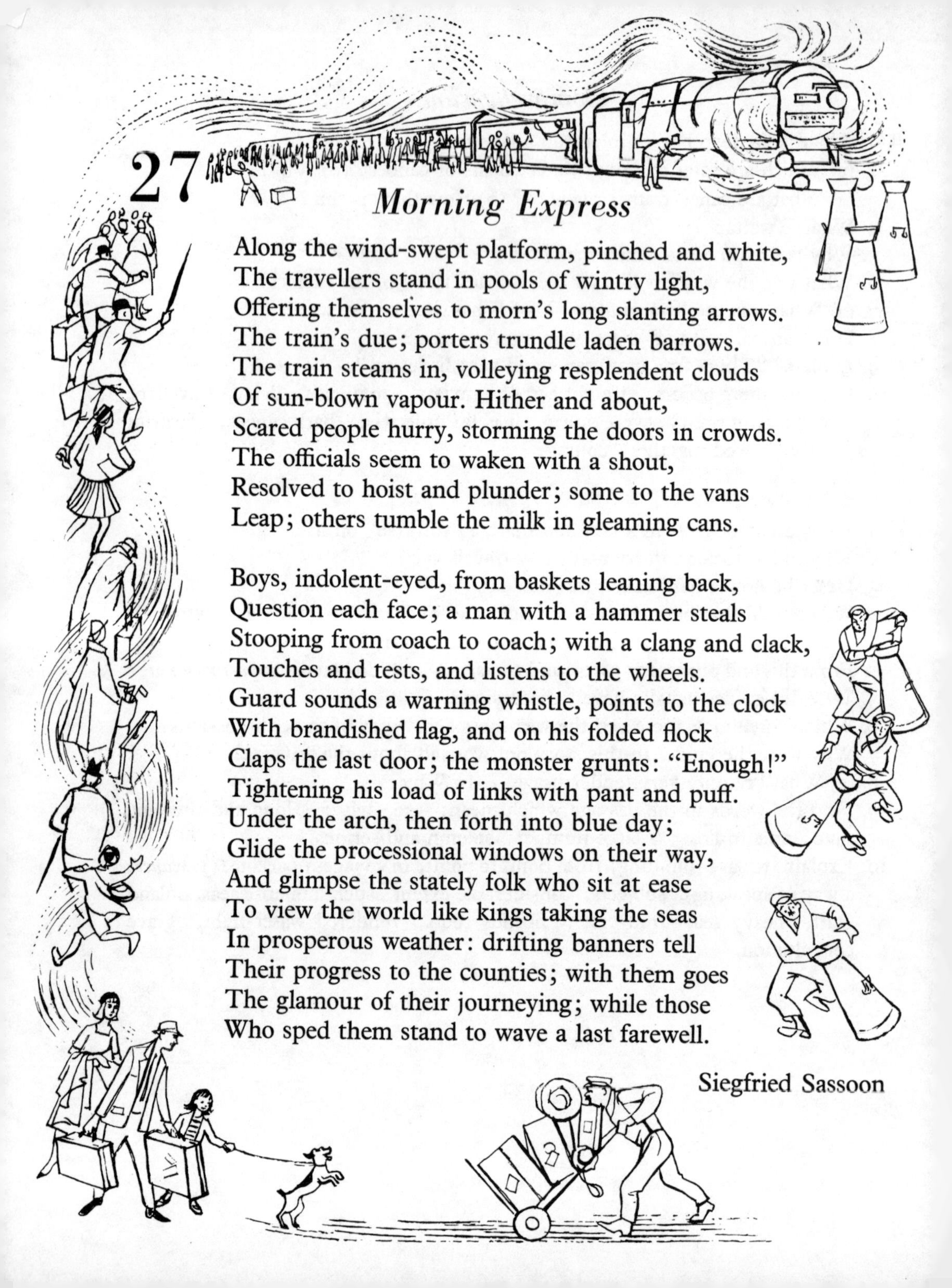

27

Morning Express

Along the wind-swept platform, pinched and white,
The travellers stand in pools of wintry light,
Offering themselves to morn's long slanting arrows.
The train's due; porters trundle laden barrows.
The train steams in, volleying resplendent clouds
Of sun-blown vapour. Hither and about,
Scared people hurry, storming the doors in crowds.
The officials seem to waken with a shout,
Resolved to hoist and plunder; some to the vans
Leap; others tumble the milk in gleaming cans.

Boys, indolent-eyed, from baskets leaning back,
Question each face; a man with a hammer steals
Stooping from coach to coach; with a clang and clack,
Touches and tests, and listens to the wheels.
Guard sounds a warning whistle, points to the clock
With brandished flag, and on his folded flock
Claps the last door; the monster grunts: "Enough!"
Tightening his load of links with pant and puff.
Under the arch, then forth into blue day;
Glide the processional windows on their way,
And glimpse the stately folk who sit at ease
To view the world like kings taking the seas
In prosperous weather: drifting banners tell
Their progress to the counties; with them goes
The glamour of their journeying; while those
Who sped them stand to wave a last farewell.

Siegfried Sassoon

Comprehension

A 1. Where is the platform?

2. (a) What time of day is it? (b) What time of year?
3. What is the weather like?
4. What are the porters doing?
5. In the poem there are vans, baskets, coaches, wheels, links and windows. Give each noun an adjective of your own.
6. What is in shining churns?
7. (a) What is the man with the hammer doing? (b) Why?
8. (a) What is the "warning whistle"? (b) Why is it blown?
9. (a) What monster is there? (b) Why is *monster* a good name for it?
10. Explain: wind-swept, travellers, trundle laden barrows, crowds, drifting, brandished, folk, hither and about, storming the doors, seem to waken.

B 1. (a) Who look pale and cold? (b) Why?

2. Why are people scared?
3. (a) Describe the boys. (b) Why do you think they have baskets?
4. How can windows be processional?
5. (a) Who are the stately folk? (b) Why are they so described?
6. (a) How can kings "take the seas"? (b) Why are they mentioned?
7. (a) What are the "drifting banners"? (b) Describe them.
8. Why should "glamour" be a very good word about travel?
9. How can we tell that the station is not an open-air one?
10. Explain: pools of wintry light, morn's long slanting arrows, volleying resplendent (shining) clouds of sun-blown vapour, the officials, resolved to hoist and plunder, indolent-eyed, question each face, brandished flag, his folded flock (why are they called this?), the monster grunts "Enough!", tightening his load of links, prosperous weather, their progress to the counties, those who sped them.

27 Language

1. (a) Use the following similes in sentences: as stubborn as a mule, as steady as a rock, as sound as a bell, as safe as houses.
   (b) Complete these similes and say when they are used: as cold as ——, as true as ——, as right as ——, as dry as ——.

2. SYNONYMS, ANTONYMS AND HOMONYMS

A word with the same (or nearly the same) meaning as another word: a synonym.
A word opposite in meaning to another word: an antonym.
More difficult to remember: Words sounding exactly the same, like *seize, seas, sees,* (not just rhymes) are called homonyms.
Remember: A synonym or an antonym must be *the same part of speech* as its partner: the synonym or antonym of an adjective must be another adjective, etc.
WEALTH (noun) synonym: riches (noun) antonym: poverty (noun)

(a) What are the antonyms of: indolent, question, stooping, prosperous, farewell, wintry, offering, laden, hoist, tightening?
(b) Give synonyms of: indolent, question, prosperous, farewell, resolved, plunder, hoist, leap, gleaming, banners.
(c) Think of homonyms of: morn's, seem, eyed, steal, links, seas, wave, phrase, piece, pier, place, plain, pour, practice, praise, pray, prize.

Give the meaning of your words in (c).

3. *Find the Stranger* windswept vapour wintry white blue last

4. (a) Complete this table:

	Gender		*Home*	*Young*	*Any Collective Nouns*
Common	*Masculine*	*Feminine*			
people (human beings)	man (father)	woman (mother)	house, etc.	child	a crowd, etc., of people
horse	——	——	——	——	a string of ——
					a team of ——
fowls	——	——	——	——	a —— of chicks
pig	——	——	——	——	a —— of piglets
cattle	——	——	——	——	a —— of ——
lion	——	——	——	——	a ——
wolf	——	——	——	——	a ——

(b) What are leverets, elvers, cygnets, goslings and fawns?

5. *Business Letters* When we write to a firm (perhaps to order something) or to someone who is not a friend or a relation, we begin and end our letter like this:

Dear Sir, (OR Dear Madam,)

Yours faithfully,
J. Smith

If the letter is to a man, the address on the envelope will begin: E. Jones, Esq. Draw an envelope and address it to your father, as part of a business letter.

6. (a) Which words in the poem rhyme with light, barrows, crowds, wheels, seas?
   (b) Which of these words rhymes with WEIGHED: play, paid, white, sighed?
7. Complete this table:

train	station	platform	compartments	passengers	journey
ship	——	——	——	——	——

8. Select a suitable word from those in the brackets to make sensible sentences:
   (i) An (old, ancient, antique) man was climbing (slowly, swiftly, frenziedly) up the (flat, grassy, steep) path to his (palace, mansion, cottage).
   (ii) "I'm (afraid, frightened, nervous, terrified) I can't swim very well," I said.
   (iii) The express (roared, whispered, stopped) out of the (points, track, tunnel, bridge) and went (past, passed) us like (lightening, lightning).
9. Write three sentences, using *arch* as a noun, verb and adjective.
10. What do you wish to know if you enquire at a railway station about (a) arrivals (b) departures?
11. What do we find in these: timetable, atlas, reference book, catalogue, encyclopaedia, telephone directory, library, museum, greenhouse?
12. Write correctly:
    hurry along there please shouted the guard of our train youre too busy looking at the flying scotsman said my father crossly come along now or we shall miss our train i know its a pity you dont have the chance every day to see a famous express thats why i was looking i said perhaps i shall see it when we come back to london
13. Describe what people are doing when they are skating, tobogganing, ski-ing, swimming, drowning, camping, stalking, veering, tacking (2), persevering, trespassing, poaching, mimicking, chastising, repairing, scrutinising, terrorising.
14. *Spelling* (a) inside: int . . . . l (b) outside: . . . . l (c) everlasting: e . . . . . l (d) left over: sur . . . . (e) signs standing for something: sym . . . . (f) tell the difference: dist . . . . (g) disappeared: v . . . . (h) was successful: suc . . . . . . (i) cannot be resisted: irr . . . . (j) disorder: ch . . .

15. Describe each person's work: forester, explorer, weaver, collier, conjuror, porter, engineer, docker, gamekeeper, auctioneer, solicitor, lawyer, warder.
16. Use in sentences: wind-swept platform travellers wintry light sun-blown vapour gleaming cans a warning whistle monster "Enough!"

Find Out

1. Find what these words mean, then use one from each group in sentences:
   hurry, harry, harass, embarrass flag, flock, fold, enfold, refold
   volley, valley, volume, voluble, volunteer, voluntary, involve, revolve
   journey, journal, adjourn, adjoin, adjacent, adjust station, stationary, stationery
   procession, process, proceed, precede, preside indolent, indignant, industrious.
2. Find the meaning of: bring to light, hide one's light under a bushel, as light as a feather or ——, light-fingered, light-hearted, light-headed, make light of it, throw light on a problem, light sleeper, lightning, lightening, lighthouse, lightship; head in the clouds, under a cloud, a cloudburst, cloud-capped, When the clouds roll by, Every cloud has a silver lining.
3. *Touching* Make a list of verbs of touch, like tap, rap, batter.
   Give the meaning of the words.
4. *Railways* Find out about British Railways: the regions, the chief towns served, the history of railways.
   What were or are the following: Puffing Billy, the Rocket, B.R., the Flying Scotsman, Royal Scot, Red Dragon, Cornish Riviera Express, Golden Arrow, termini, St. Pancras, Victoria, Waterloo?

List of Poems

Morning Express by Siegfried Sassoon.
Night Mail by W. H. Auden.
The Railway Junction by Walter de la Mare.
The Night Express by Cosmo Monkhouse.
The Express by Stephen Spender.
Adlestrop by Edward Thomas.
Locomotive by Emily Dickinson.
The Child in the Train by Eleanor Farjeon.
From a Railway Carriage by Robert Louis Stevenson.

Comprehension comes at the end of this exercise.

28 *Language*

1. (a) What do these words mean: synonym, antonym, homonym?
   (b) Give the synonyms of alarmed, swarmed up, talking, hurried glance, see;
   the antonyms of visibly, coming, right (2), ugly, less;
   the homonyms of I, I'll, hour, sight, be, profit, key, choir.
2. COMMON EXPRESSIONS OR SAYINGS In the Comprehension extract, "Chased by the Navy", there are these common sayings: looking very ugly, turned visibly white to the lips, in a hole, up a tree, in the road, a mighty close call.
   These sayings are not strictly true, as no one was in an actual hole, etc. They are common expressions to describe something in a vivid, interesting way.
   (a) Give their meaning.
   (b) What do we mean when we use the following expressions or sayings?
      (i) Oh, he's *a wet blanket* and will never join in.
      (ii) The whole class was *under a cloud* until the culprit confessed.
      (iii) Now we are both *in the same boat* and must help each other to escape.
      (iv) Those two are always *at loggerheads*.
      (v) After years of enmity the two men decided to *bury the hatchet*.
      (vi) John Smith's workmates *sent* him *to Coventry* for refusing to join the strike.
      (vii) Winning first prize was *a feather in his cap*.
      (viii) He became so tired in the swimming race that he *threw up the sponge*.
      (ix) It's time you *turned over a new leaf* and behaved properly.
   (c) What are these: a blind-alley job, a flash in the pan (why?), dead beat, face the music, every man Jack, a busman's holiday (why?)?
   Remember: Common sayings used in free-and-easy speech are called *colloquialisms*.
3. *Find the Stranger* stunsails frigates mainmast topsails helm
4. What is wrong in this sentence: "There's three frigates coming down."?
5. Say what these sentences mean:
   (i) The cutter's bearing up to close. (ii) The cutter's too close.
   Use *close* in three sentences as a verb, an adjective and a noun.
6. *Spelling* (a) of different kinds: v . . . . us (b) a group of people: com . . . . . e
   (c) gathered together: ass . . . . . . (d) opposite of ancestors: des . . . .
   (e) manual skill: dex . . . . . . (f) full of skill: ski . . . l (g) usual: cus . . . . . .

(h) covering: v . . l . . g (i) unceasingly: inc . . . . (j) eternally: perp . . . .

7. (a) What is thc mcaning given by the suffix: otherwise, windward, cutter, smuggler, duckling, granary, student, blameless, graceful, tigress?

   (b) What is the meaning given by the prefix: illegal, impossible, incorrect, irregular, ashore, abstract, anteroom, bicycle, circumference, disagree?

8. Write correctly:

   (i) I have read these (to, two, too) books and think this is the (better, best) one.

   (ii) (Who, Whom) did you find in the cellar?

   (iii) I dislike (that, those) kind of apples.

   (iv) He (don't, does not) (no, now, know) (nothing, anything) about the matter.

   (v) There will be a football (practice, practise) tonight.

   (vi) The car (run, ran) (in, into) the back of the (stationery, stationary) bus.

   (vii) Each of us (say, says) that the girl is a (hero, heroine).

   (viii) "Please (can, may) I (lend, borrow) this book ("?, ?") Jean asked politely.

9. Complete this table:

helmsman, ship, steer	:	——, car, ——	:	drover, ——, ——
yacht, sails (noun)	:	steamship, ——	:	electric train, ——
three pounds, six pounds	:	single, ——	:	fifty, ——
rope, string	:	——, path	:	river, ——

10. (a) What is the difference between an aviary and an apiary?

    (b) Where are wild animals kept in captivity? (c) Where do orphans live?

    (d) Where are the following kept or stored: aeroplanes, cars, gas, grain?

    (e) Where do we go to see (i) pictures (ii) films (iii) our doctor (iv) our Government (v) coal mining (vi) children being educated?

11. Give (i) the Simple Past, (ii) the Past tense with "have": write, weave, wear, tread, throw, tear, take, swim, strike, spring.

12. Suffix *or*, *er*: What do we call a person who travels, does conjuring tricks, trains football teams, wrestles, boxes, visits, is in debt, writes stories, invents, does jobs for the teacher?

13. (a) Change to Indirect Speech:

    "That shows they have information," said Marah grimly, "otherwise they'd not be looking for us here."

    (b) Change to Direct Speech:

    Marah told Jim that he was afraid they would be captured.

14. Put into alphabetical order: this, time, the, two, train, to, that, too, top.
15. Describe each action: tap, rap, knock, batter, bruise, squeeze, squash, hit, stroke, rub, smite, tickle, touch, punch, seize, hold, grasp.
16. Use in sentences: smugglers hand-swivel guns Salcombe boat grimly information signalled ten miles from home a curious whanging whine.

Find Out

1. Find what these words mean, then use one from each group in sentences:
   pressed, compressed, depressed, impressed, expressed, repressed, suppressed
   signalled, signaller, signature, signed, sighed, sighted, sited
   visible, invisible, invincible, divisible information, informal
   evidently, evidence curious, curio probably, possibly.
2. Find the meaning of: Navy blue; a cutter, cutlery, cutler, cutlass, cut and dried plans, cut and thrust, short cut, cut a caper, cut a dash, cut and come again, cut away, cut down, cut it fine, cut one's teeth, cut short, cut to pieces, a cut-purse, cut-throat, cutting.
3. *Poetry 2* Find Rudyard Kipling's poem, "A Smuggler's Song", and use it to help you to write your own poem about smuggling.
4. *Pirates and Smugglers* Find out about famous pirates and about smuggling. Make a list of different words for "pirate", like *corsair*.
   Who were the Vikings, Barbary pirates, the English Elizabethan "pirates", Captain Morgan, Captain Kidd, William Dampier?
   Explain: walking the plank, keel-hauling, hanging from the yard-arm, the Customs.

Book List

Jim Davis by John Masefield.
Thunder in the Bay by Adrian Seligman.
Moonfleet by J. Meade Falkner.
The Sea Rover; The King's Corsair; Companions of Fortune by René Guillot.
The Ship Aground; The Valiant Sailor by C. Fox Smith.
He Sailed with Blackbeard by Frank Knight.
From Faeroes to Finisterre by John Merrett.
Pirates, Pirates, Pirates edited by Phyllis R. Fenner.
The True Book about Smugglers and Smuggling by Leonard Gribble.

28 *Chased by the Navy*

By this time the other smugglers had become alarmed. The longboat gun, which worked on a slide abaft all, was cleared, and the two little cohorns, or hand-swivel guns, which pointed over the sides, were trained and loaded. A man swarmed up the mainmast to look around. "The cutter's bearing up to close," he called out. "I see she's the Salcombe boat."

"That shows they have information," said Marah grimly, "otherwise they'd not be looking for us here. Someone has been talking to his wife." He hailed the masthead again. "Have the frigates seen us yet?"

For answer, the man took a hurried glance to windward, turned visibly white to the lips, and slid down a rope to the deck. "Bearing down fast, under stunsails," he reported. "The cutter's signalled them with her topsail. There's three frigates coming down," he added.

"Right," said Marah. "I'll go up and see for myself."

He went up, and came down again looking very ugly. He evidently thought that he was in a hole. "As she goes," he called to the helmsman, "get all you can on the sheets, boys. Now, Jim, you're up a tree; you're within an hour of being pressed into the Navy. How'd ye like to be a ship's boy, hey, and get tickled up by a bo'sun's rope-end?"

"I shouldn't like it at all," I answered.

"You'll like it a jolly sight less than that," said he, "and it's what you'll probably be. We're ten miles from home. The cutter's in the road. The frigates will be on us in half-an-hour. It will be a mighty close call, my son; we shall have to fight to get clear."

At the instant of time something went overhead with a curious whanging whine.

"That's a three-pound ball," said Marah, pointing to a spurt upon a wave. "The cutter wants us to stop and have breakfast with 'em."

From *Jim Davis* by John Masefield

Comprehension

A 1. (a) Who had become worried? (b) Why?
2. Why did a man climb up the tallest mast?
3. (a) From which port did the cutter come? (b) What are two meanings of *cutter*?
4. In which direction were the frigates?
5. How did the look-out man come down again?
6. Insert two words: The cutter had signalled to the —— ——.
7. (a) Who went aloft to see for himself? (b) Why do you think he did this?
8. How far were the smugglers from home?
9. (a) What went over their boat? (b) Why?
10. Explain: smugglers, worked on a slide, grimly, hailed, evidently, you're within an hour . . ., tickled up by a bo'sun's rope-end.

B 1. (a) What were cohorns? (b) What did the smugglers do with them?
2. What is the difference between training a gun and training a dog?
3. Complete: The smugglers' boat was a ——, the Salcombe boat was a —— and the Naval boats were ——.
4. (a) What showed that someone had talked to his wife? (b) How did it show this?
5. How long would it take the frigates to reach the smugglers?
6. Who do you think Marah was? NOT simply "a smuggler".
7. What do you think Marah meant when he said "The cutter wants us to stop and have breakfast with 'em."?
8. Why was there a sudden splash in the sea?
9. What was the *full name* of the boy who might have to join the Navy?
10. Explain: abaft all (*aft* means "towards the *stern*"), the longboat gun . . . was cleared, hand-swivel guns, swarmed up the mainmast, a hurried glance to windward, turned visibly white to the lips, bearing down fast, looking very ugly, in a hole, get all you can on the sheets, you're up a tree, pressed into the Navy, in the road, a mighty close call, three-pound ball.

29 *The Chase*

The fourth evening found them on their way again, after a day spent lying-up in a thicket of thorn-trees. A murky evening, closing in under a low grey sky. In the low country at their backs it was dusk already, but up here on the high moors the daylight still lingered, reflected back by many little silver tarns among the brown heather.

"Three more days," Marcus said suddenly. "Three more days by my reckoning, and we should reach the Wall!"

Esca looked round to answer, and then suddenly his head went up with a jerk, as though he heard something. An instant later, Marcus heard it too, very faint and far behind: a hound giving tongue.

They had reached the crest of a long ridge of moorland, and looking back, they saw a cluster of dark specks cresting a lesser ridge behind them; a long way behind, but not too far to be recognized for what they were: men on horseback and many hounds. And in that instant another hound took up the cry.

"I spoke too soon," Marcus said, and his voice jumped oddly in his own ears.

"They have sighted us," Esca laughed sharply in his throat. "The hunt is up with a vengeance. Ride, brother quarry!" And even as he spoke, his little mount leapt forward, snorting, from the jab of his heel.

Marcus urged his own pony into a tearing gallop at the same instant. The ponies were fairly fresh, but both fugitives knew that in the open it was only a matter of time before they were ridden down by the better-mounted tribesmen—pulled down by the yelling hounds as by a pack of wolves. And with one accord they swung a little in their course, heading for the higher ground ahead; broken country by the look of it, in which they might be able to shake off their pursuers.

"If we can keep the lead till dark," Esca shouted above the drumming hooves and the wind of their going, "we've a chance among the glens yonder."

From *The Eagle of the Ninth* by Rosemary Sutcliff

Comprehension

The Eagle of the Ninth is a story set in Roman Britain.

A 1. How many days had they been travelling?
2. What did they do on the fourth day?
3. Were they on a mountain peak, in a deep valley or on high moorland?
4. How long did one man think it would take them to reach the Wall?
5. What were the names of the two men?
6. (a) Why did one man turn his head suddenly? (b) What was his name?
7. What did they see in the distance?
8. Why did the two men gallop away?
9. What was their only chance of escape?
10. Explain: lying-up, a thicket, murky, dusk, high moors, on their way again, reflected, heather, went up with a jerk, recognised, hounds, sighted us, mount, the jab of his heel, fairly fresh, shake off their pursuers, fugitives, tribesmen.

B 1. Why did they spend the fourth day in the way they did?
2. What was the weather like, that evening?
3. What was the first warning of the approach of the horsemen?
4. Marcus was a Roman soldier in Britain. (a) What was the Wall? (b) Why did they want to reach it?
If you do not know the answers, try to guess sensibly.
5. (*a*) What did Marcus mean by: "I spoke too soon"? (b) Why did his voice jump oddly?
6. (a) Why did Esca call Marcus "brother quarry"? (b) What other *quarry* do you know?
7. Why did they change course?
8. Why would they have a chance of escape in the glens?
9. How could it be dusk in the lowlands and still daylight on the moors?
10. Explain: closing in, low country at their backs, daylight still lingered, tarns, by my reckoning, the crest, cresting a lesser ridge, in the open, ridden down, better-mounted, with one accord, broken country, the wind of their going, the eagle of the Ninth Legion (guess sensibly).
Find out the meaning of: The hunt is up with a vengeance.

29 Language

1. What do we mean when we say: mind your p's and q's, send someone packing, turn the tables on someone, lead someone a dance, haul someone over the coals, strike while the iron's hot, have forty winks, play with fire, come a cropper, have pins and needles, a storm in a teacup?

2. MORE ABOUT NOUNS In the Comprehension extract, "The Chase", are the nouns *pursuers* and *hunt*.

   pursuers: the persons who do the action *pursuit*: the name of the action
   hunters: the persons who do the action *hunt* or *hunting*: the name of the action

   (a) Complete this table:

Name of Action	"*Doer*" (name of one who does the action)
exploration	——
advice	——
plumbing	——
——	visitor
——	traveller

   (b) Names of places, etc., may be included, besides names of actions: empire, emperor; farm, farmer.

   Give the persons to fit these places: England, Holland, mountain, colliery, village, city, vicarage, smithy.

3. *Spelling* (a) like a black shadow: sil....... (b) happening together: sim.........ly (c) wild killing: sla...... (d) unable to speak: spe....... (e) not capable: ..eff...... (f) false belief: del..... (g) complicated: ela...... (h) always prying: inq........ (i) cold cupboard: ref......... (j) very hardworking: cons.........

4. Give homonyms of: days, heel, were, might, profit, quay, rain, raise, rap, red. Give the meaning of your words.

5. *Find the Strangers*
   (a) thicket crest mountain ridge
   (b) evening day dusk night moonlight morning
   (c) little fresh higher dark faint low
   (d) looked said recognised spoke shake leapt
   (e) days thorn-trees dusk tarns specks hounds

6. Find the errors in this request: Can I lend your pencil-sharpener?

7. Some words can be spelt with S or Z: recognized, recognised.
   S is the more modern spelling.
   Use recognise and two other ISE verbs in sentences.
8. (a) Give the singular of tarns, wolves, pursuers, fugitives, knives, ponies, they, tribesmen, hooves, measles, billiards, spectacles.
   (b) Give the plural of country, cry, brother, loaf, cargo, halo, piano, tomato, chimney, lady, echo, sheep, trout, salmon.
9. (a) Give synonyms of: answer, instantly, men on horseback, hounds, jumped.
   (b) Give antonyms of: fresh, murky, faint, far, scared, easy, lazily, tight.
10. Write the following, then underline the pronouns, write V over the verbs, ADV over the adverbs, ADJ over the adjectives, N over the nouns and PREP over prepositions: "They have sighted us." Esca laughed sharply in his throat . . . his little mount leapt forward . . .
11. What do we call the young of: bears, goats, pigs, deer, hares, cattle, horses, elephants, swans, dogs, foxes, ducks, fowls, tigers, cats, frogs, eagles, humans, royalty, lions?
12. What do we call a native of Holland, Switzerland, Wales, Scotland, Austria, Fiji, Tonga, South Africa, Nigeria, Egypt, Germany, Italy, U.S.A.?
13. Complete these collective nouns: a galaxy or constellation of ——, a —— of stairs, a clutch of ——, a fleet of —— (2), a suite of —— (2).
14. Explain the meaning and use of these similes: as poor as a churchmouse, as changeable as the weather, as cool as a cucumber, as dull as ditchwater, as dead as a doornail, as easy as winking, as fresh as a daisy, as pure as the driven snow.
15. (a) Add suitable subjects (*long phrases*, not just "The man", "The boy", etc.) to:
    (i) ———— rowed out to the fishing-grounds.
    (ii) ———— climbed slowly and cautiously up the crags.
    (b) Add suitable objects, as in (a):
    (i) The brave soldier defended ————.
    (ii) The dappled fawn stared fearfully at ————.
    (iii) The carpenter broke ————.
16. Write correctly:
    exercise 29 comprehension extract the chase comes from the eagle of the ninth a story about roman britain by rosemary sutcliff in the extract marcus and esca are being pursued by hostile tribesmen in caledonia which is now called scotland

17. What is a compound word? Name five and say whether they are nouns or adjectives.
18. Use in sentences: the fourth evening a thicket of thorn-trees dusk little silver tarns a cluster of dark specks moorland the jab of his heel the eagle of the Ninth.

Find Out

1. Find what these words mean, then use one from each group in sentences:
   forward, foreword, prologue, epilogue fourth, forth, Firth of Forth
   country, countryside, county, continent, contentment, contents, contempt
   tarn, tarnished, tarpaulin, tartan, tarry, tardy, tawdry (origin?), tawny
   specks, spectacle, spectacles, spectre, sceptre, except, accept.
2. Find the meaning of: close at one's heels, show a clean pair of heels, cool one's heels, down at heel, take to one's heels, head over heels, come to heel, lay by the heels, turn on one's heel, heel over; speak tongue in cheek, keep a civil tongue in one's head, hold one's tongue, a sharp tongue, tongue-tied, a shoe tongue, the tongue of a bell.
3. *Land* Make a list of words containing *land*, like landlady, woodland, moorland. Give the meaning of the words.
4. *The History of Britain* Put these into their proper time-order, then find out something about each one: Danish invaders, Ancient Britons, Queen Victoria, Drake, the Invasion of Normandy, the Great Fire of London, Angles and Saxons, Hadrian's Wall, the Battle of Hastings, QE2, the Ascent of Everest.

Book List

The Eagle of the Ninth; The Lantern Bearers; The Silver Branch; Mark of the Horse Lord by Rosemary Sutcliff.
Word to Caesar by Geoffrey Trease.
Legions of the Eagle by Henry Treece.
Two Young Explorers by Margaret Black.
Bronze Eagles by Joan Selby-Lowndes.
They Fought for Brigantia by M. A. Rowling.
Roman Eagle, Celtic Hawk by E. A. Gray.
The True Book about Roman Britain by Patrick Moore.
The Romans Were Here by Jack Lindsay.
Our Homeland in the Dark Ages by W. J. Claxton.

Comprehension comes at the end of this exercise.

30 *Language*

1. Give the persons who fit these nouns, like farm, *farmer*; violin, *violinist*:
   collection, deceit, discovery, Italy, attendance, assistance, friendship, science.
2. COMPOUND WORDS When two words are joined together to make a new word, we call the new word a *compound word*: chest, nut: chestnut.

   Remember: If the new word is an adjective, there is usually a hyphen: sea-green.

   (a) Find eight Compound words in the Comprehension poem and say whether each one is a noun, adjective or adverb.

   (b) Form compound words by joining pairs from this list:
   hard, heavy, table, pot, ache, grand, tooth, cloth, head, man, weight, tea, father, brush, green, working, sea, milk.

   (c) Complete these compound words: ——house, ——bird, ——ball, ink——, church——, moon——.

   Use in sentences a compound word from (a), (b) and (c).
3. *Find the Stranger* fox-red chestnut beanstalk parchment runway.
4. Choose the word which means *most* angry, *most* afraid, etc.:
   (i) The squirrel was (angry, cross, annoyed, enraged, indignant, resentful).
   (ii) The mouse was (terrified, afraid, scared, frightened, alarmed, disturbed).
   (iii) The children were (happy, glad, gleeful, cheerful, pleased, overjoyed).
   (iv) The prisoners were (unhappy, melancholy, broken-hearted, sad).
   (v) The light was (bright, glowing, shining, twinkling, brilliant, beaming).
   (vi) The North wind was (cold, chilly, freezing, wintry, keen, cool).
5. (a) Where do you find an aisle?
   (b) Use in sentences two other words which sound exactly the same as "aisle".
   (c) What do we call words which sound exactly the same?
   (d) What do we call words of similar meaning?
   (e) What do we call words of opposite meaning?
6. *Spelling* (a) tilling the land: cul........ (b) plenty (noun): abu...... (c) advise when someone is choosing: rec...... (d) spoken memories: remi......... (e) keep trying: per...... (f) not noticeable: incon........ (g) very great: cons ...... le (h) noun from *probable*: p .... (i) what one decides to do: res .... (j) red soreness: inf ....

7. Think of homonyms of right, ring, road, root, sealing, serial, sold, sword, stationery, thrown. Give the meaning of your words.
8. Use in sentences: bough, bought, brought, borrow.
9. In what way is the poem, "The Squirrel", like "A Summer Noon" in Exercise 23?
10. What is an apostrophe? Give an example of its use (i) showing ownership and (ii) to make an abbreviation.
11. Give the meaning of these words, using your dictionary if necessary: accumulate adversity affirmative aggravate ambiguous camouflage guarantee menagerie peninsula rheumatism dissatisfaction opportunity.
12. (a) What do we call the punctuation marks at the end of the following lines of the poem: lines 2, 3, 4, the next to the last line, the last line?

    Say when we use each one. What other punctuation marks do we use?

    (b) Write this correctly:

    i surprised a squirrel among the fox red fallen leaves. But it ran away catch me if you can he seemed to shout chattering angrily
13. (a) What do we find in the following: zoo, aviary, apiary, two kinds of nursery, reservoir, garage, museum, Art Gallery, laundry, barracks, dry dock, aquarium, granary, studio (several kinds), building sites?

    (b) Where do these sports take place: boxing, athletics, bowls, golf, skating?
14. Complete these similes and say when we might use each one:

    as —— as a hunter, as —— as two peas, as —— as a new pin, as —— as a lamb, as —— as Job, as —— as Punch, as —— as a peacock, as —— as brass, as —— as a post, as —— as the weather.
15. Make the second pair agree in the same way that the first pair agree:

flock, sheep	:	herd, ——
policeman, thief	:	gamekeeper, ——
man, feet	:	horse, ——
piano, pianos	:	echo, ——
wolf, cub	:	elephant, ——
poor, rich	:	ancient, ——
strength, strong	:	mischief, ——
regular, irregular	:	legible, ——
pretty, prettier	:	comfortable, ——
Denmark, Dane	:	Norway, ——

16. What do these words mean: punctuation, abbreviation, direct speech, indirect

speech, rhymes, abstract nouns, verb tenses, interjections, pronouns, prepositions, comparative and superlative degree, conjunctions, gender, prefix, suffix, concord, subject and object, simile, colloquialism?

17. Use in sentences: fox-red up-swept scolded beanstalk the highest branches swings on a spray helter-skelter splash.

Find Out

1. Find what these words mean, then use one from each group in sentences:
   fur, fir, furry, fury, fiery   ancient, modern, antique, antiquated
   reviling, revealing, revelling, revolving, revising, reversing, revering
   giants' feet, giant's feet, giant feet, giant's feat   drey, dray
   parchment, parched, perches, poached, reproached, approached.
2. Find the meaning of: caught red-handed, a red herring, a red-letter day (why?), like a red rag to a bull, see red, see the red light, red tape, a Red Admiral, redbreast, redcoat, Redskin, red-hot, redden, Red Cross; turn tail, tail away, tail someone; fall back on, fall on one's feet, fall flat, fall from grace, fall out with someone, fall through, Pride goes before a fall.
3. *Feelings* Make lists of feelings, like the lists in the first four sentences of Question 4, Language, giving as many words as possible for each feeling and saying what is the difference in meaning, like this: resentful: offended, not really very angry.
4. *Squirrels* Find out about squirrels and other rodents.
   What are these: rodents, dreys, flying squirrels and flying foxes, Common Red and American Grey, the Pigmy Squirrel of ——, the Purple Giant of ——?

List of Poems

The Squirrel by Ian Serraillier.
The Squirrel by Mary Howitt.
Mouse's Nest; Summer Images by John Clare.
Garden-Lion by Evelyn Hayes.
The Sheaf by Andrew Young.
The Grey Horse by James Reeves.
Skimbleshanks: the Railway Cat by T. S. Eliot.
The Intruders; The Cat by Richard Church.
The Spotted Fawn by Phoebe Hesketh.

30

The Squirrel

Among the fox-red fallen leaves I surprised him, Snap
up the chestnut bole he leapt,
the brown leaper, clawing, up-swept:
turned on the first bough and scolded me roundly.
That's right, load me with reviling,
spit at me, swear horrible, shame me if you can.
But scared of my smiling
off and up he scurries. Now Jack's up the beanstalk
among the dizzy giants. He skips
along the highest branches, along
tree fingers slender as string,
fur tail following, to the very tips:
then leaps the aisle—
O fear he fall
a hundred times his little length!
He's over! clings, swings on a spray,
then lightly, the ghost of a mouse, against the sky traces
for me his runway of rare wonder, races
helter-skelter without pause or break
(I think of the snail—how long would he take?)
on and onward, not done yet—
his errand? some nut-plunder, you bet.
Oh he's gone!
I peer and search and strain for him, but he's gone.
I wait and watch at the giants' feet, among
the fox-red fallen leaves. One drop
of rain lands with a smart tap
on the drum, on the parchment leaf. I wait
and wait and shiver and forget . . .

A fancy: suppose the trees, so ancient, so
venerable, so rock-rooted, suddenly
heaved up their huge elephantine hooves
(O the leaves, how they'd splutter and splash
like a waterfall, a red waterfall)—suppose
they trudged away!
What would the squirrel say?

Ian Serraillier

Comprehension

A 1. (a) What was surprised among the fallen leaves?
(b) What was its name: Snap, Jack, Dizzy, It did not have a name?
2. What did it do immediately?
3. How far did it go before turning round?
4. (a) What did it do there? (b) Why?
5. (a) What are the "dizzy giants"? (b) Who was up among them?
6. Say which of these was in the chestnut tree: a mouse, a snail, a fox, Jack, giants, a drum, a squirrel, a waterfall.
7. What are "the giants' feet"?
8. (a) What colour are the leaves which are lying on the ground? (b) Why?
9. Who trudged away?
10. Explain: I surprised him, Snap, clawing, scolded me roundly, scurries, skips, tree fingers slender as string, O fear he fall, races helter-skelter, without pause or break, his errand, the parchment leaf, rock-rooted, trudged.

B 1. (a) What is "the brown leaper"? (b) Why?
2. (a) What made it climb even higher?
(b) How do we know that it was NOT in danger?
3. "Now Jack's up the beanstalk among the dizzy giants." Explain this carefully.
4. In line 12 we read: "fur tail following, to the very tips." Tips of what?
5. How far do you think the animal might fall: (a) according to the poet?
(b) approximately (roughly)?

6. (a) Why should the poet say "the ghost of a mouse"? (b) What would *you* say?
7. (a) What taps on a "drum"? (b) What is the "drum"?
   (c) Why does the poet say this?
8. What strange idea did the poet suddenly have about the trees?
9. Answer the question in the last line of the poem.
10. Explain: fox-red fallen leaves, chestnut bole, up-swept, load me with reviling, then leaps the aisle; clings, swings on a spray; against the sky traces for me his runway of rare wonder, his errand . . . nut-plunder, A fancy, huge elephantine hooves, a red waterfall.

    Look up "venerable" (if necessary) in your dictionary, then say how trees can be venerable.